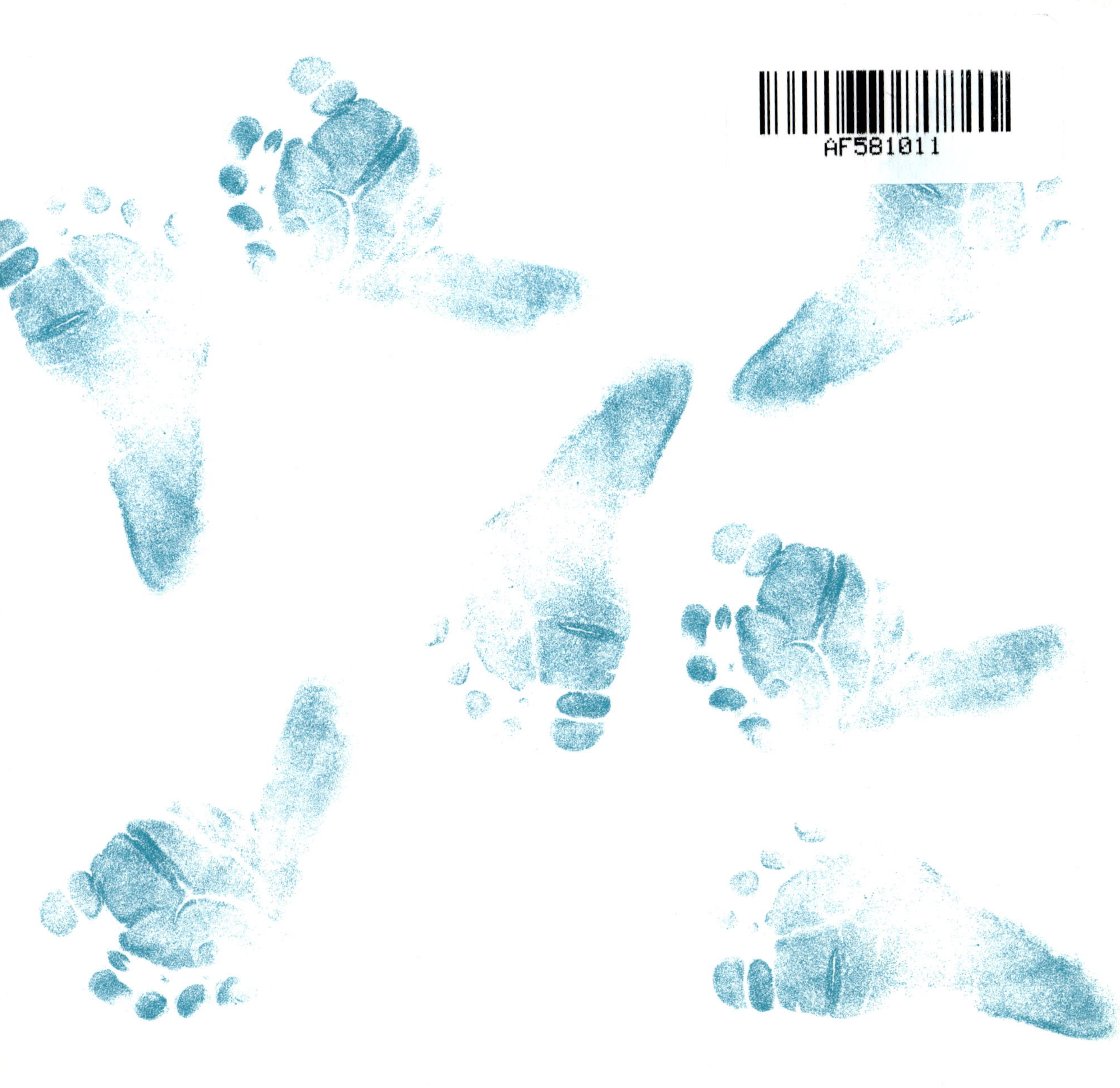

newborn

Photographs by Howard Schatz

Newborn

Project Director/Editor: Beverly Ornstein

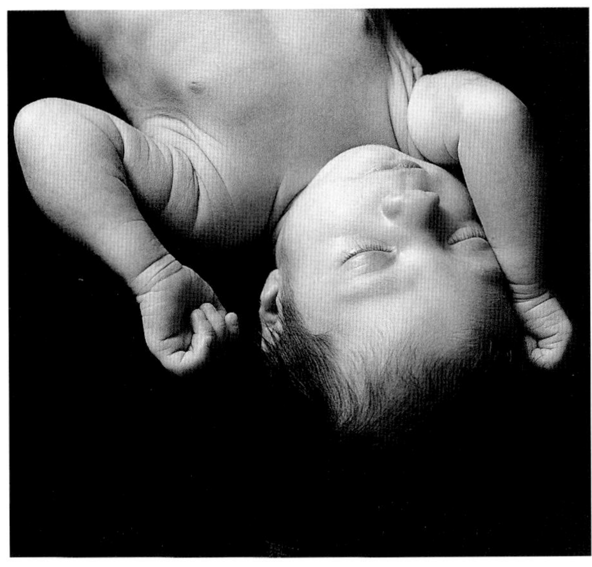

CHRONICLE BOOKS
SAN FRANCISCO

Printed in Singapore.

Book and jacket design by Pamela Geismar

Library of Congress Cataloging-in-Publication Data:
Schatz, Howard.
Newborn / photographs by Howard Schatz.
p. cm.
ISBN 0-8118-1195-6
1. Photography of infants. 2. Infants (Newborn)—Pictorial works.
I. Title.
TR681.I6S35 1996
779' .25—dc20 95-23313
CIP

title page photograph: Rebecca, 22 days

Distributed in Canada by
Raincoast Books
8680 Cambie Street
Vancouver, B.C. V6P 6M9

10 9 8 7 6 5 4 3 2 1

Chronicle Books
275 Fifth Street
San Francisco, CA 94103

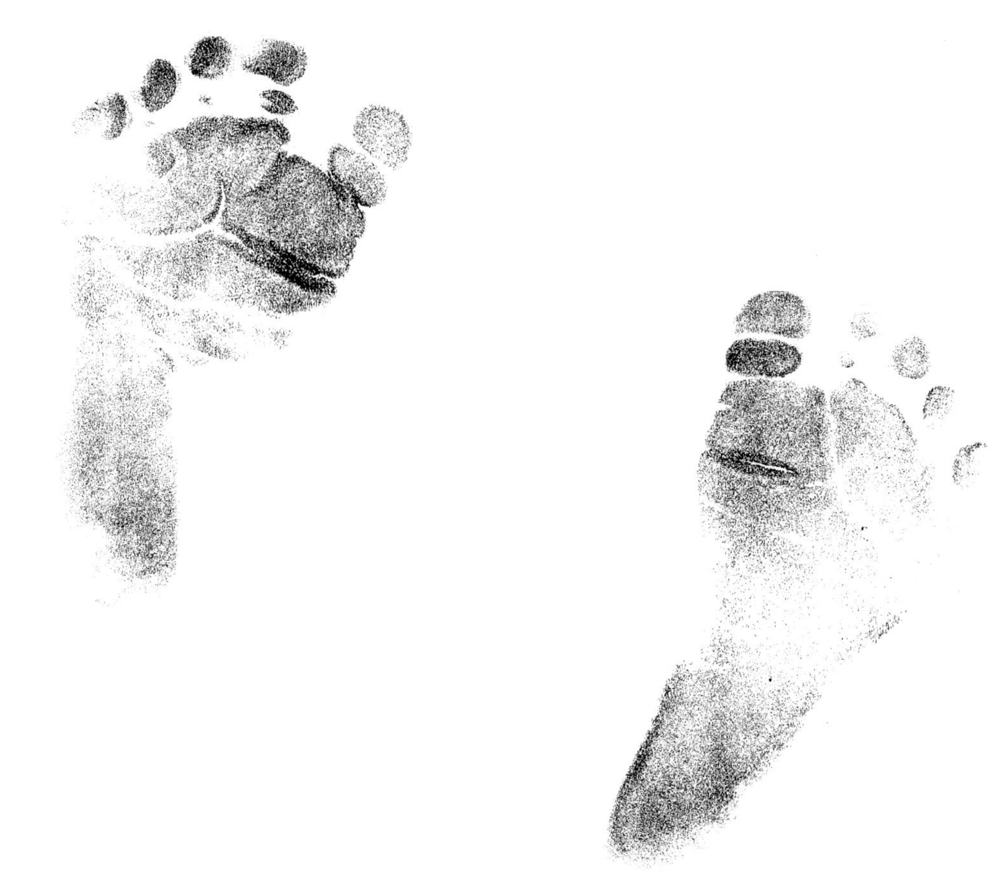

We will need to discover each step for ourselves, one feeding at a time, one crawl, one step, one school dance, one lost love, one achievement, one wrinkle. We will teach each other about life. julie winokur

8

6 days kyla

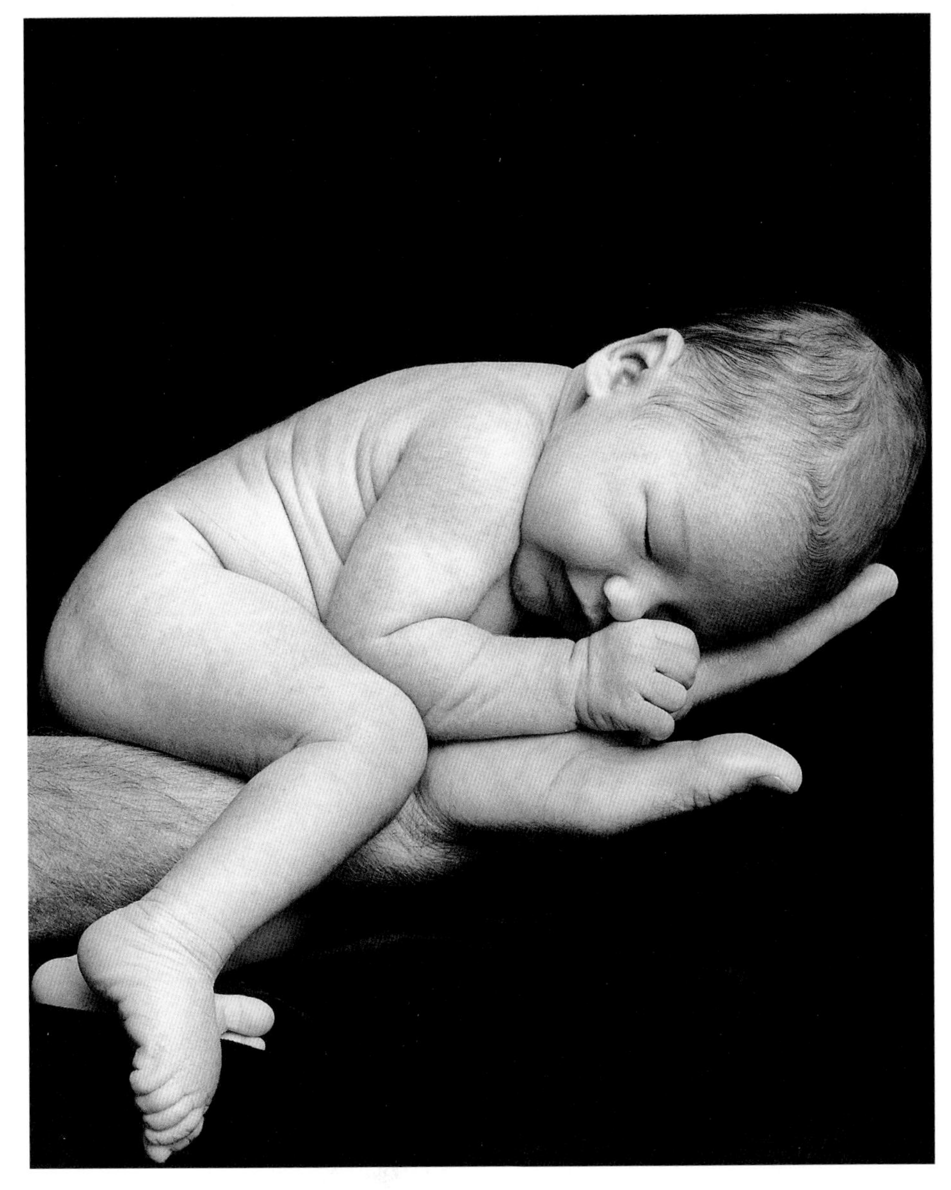

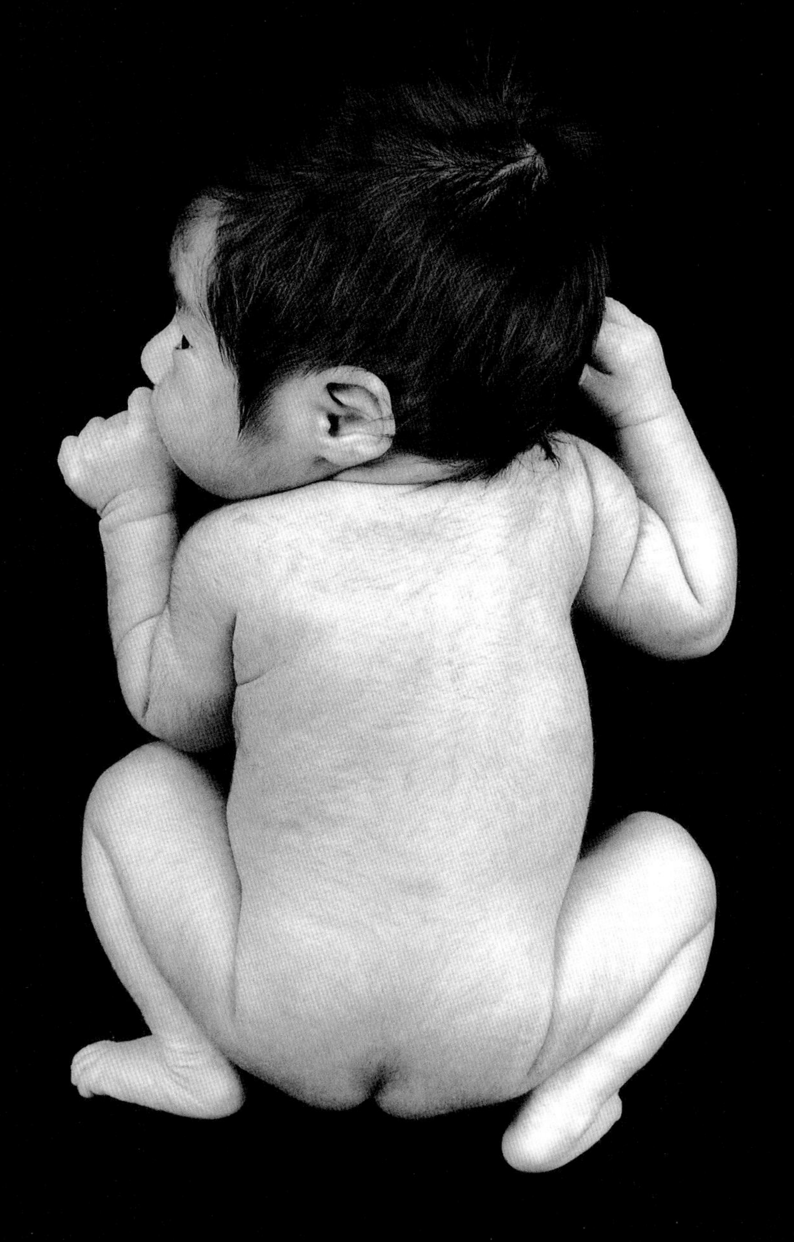

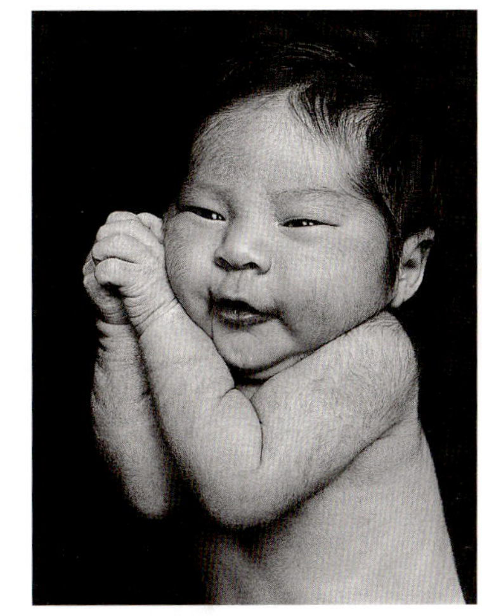

Marcus 5 days

12

Emma

3 days

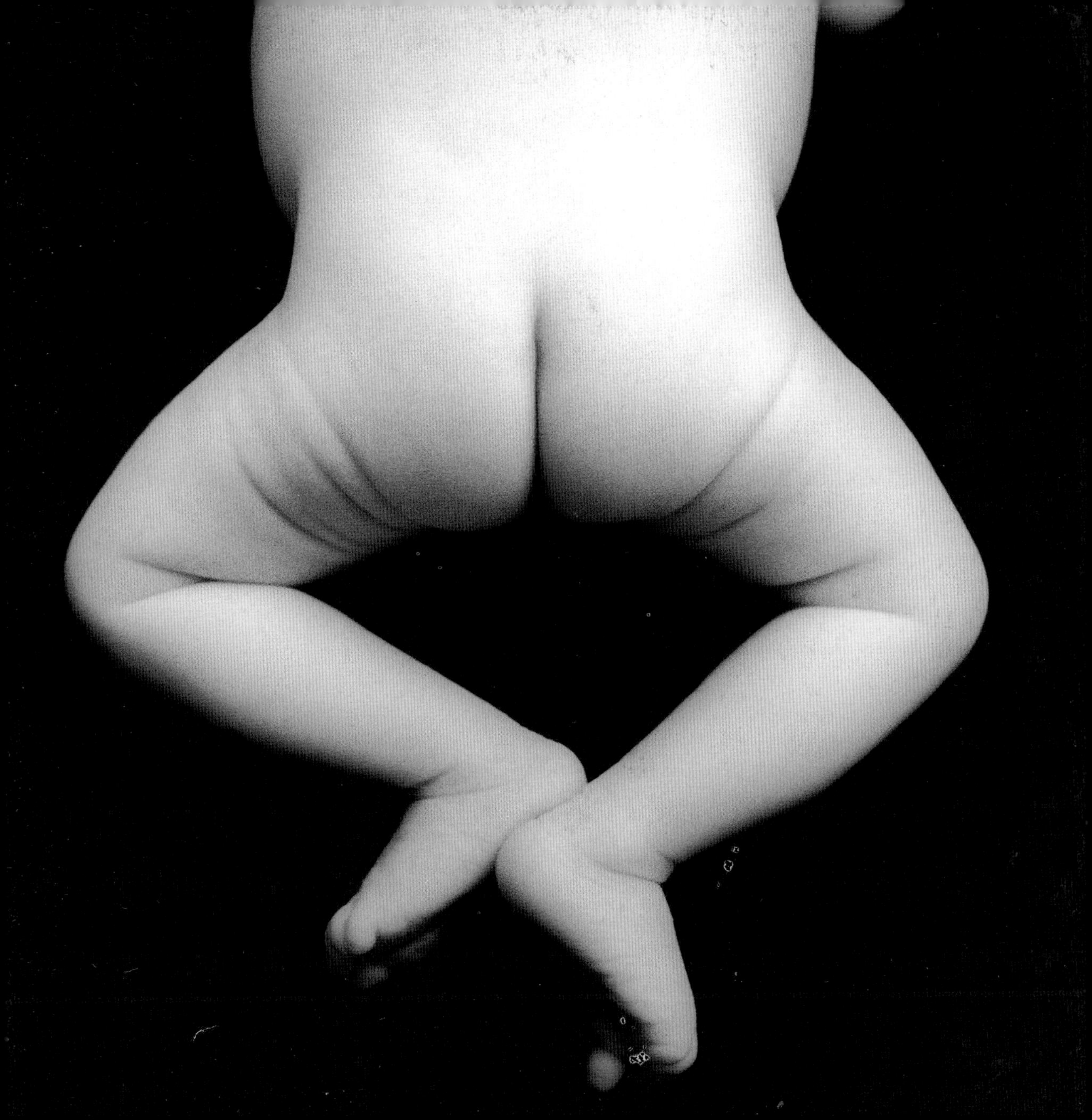

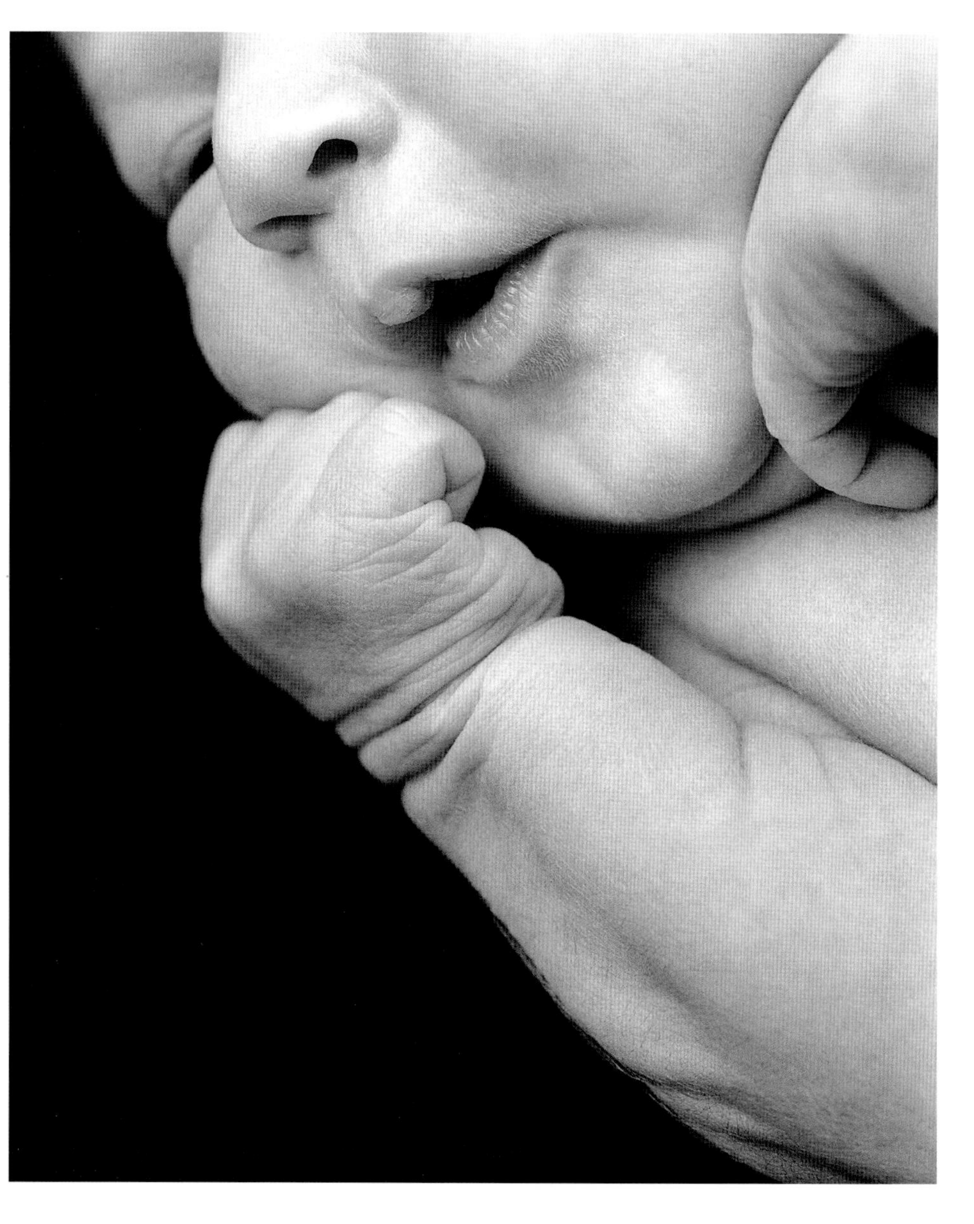

15

Ariana

1 day

2 days **charles**

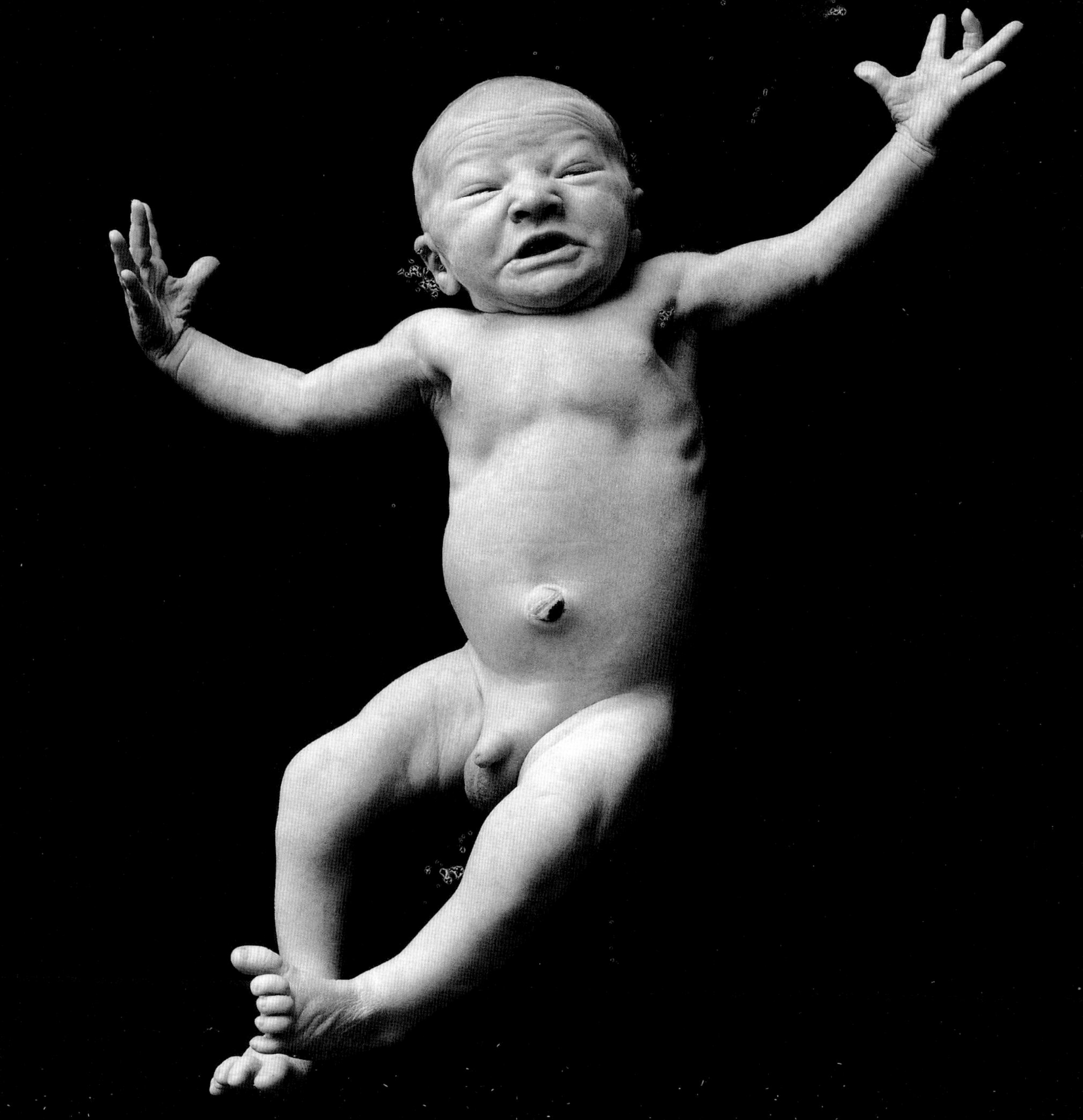

Alexa and caylin

18 days

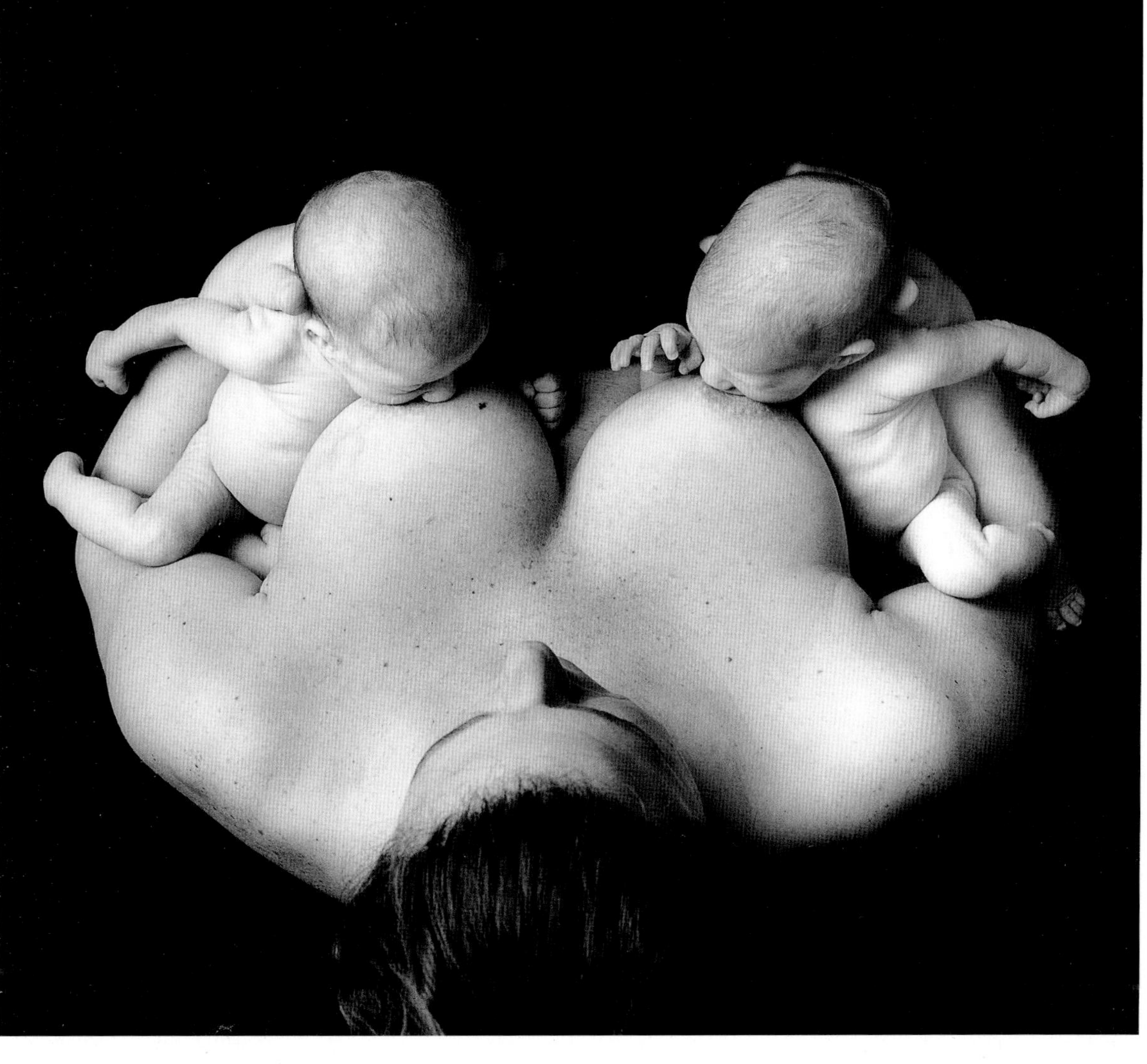

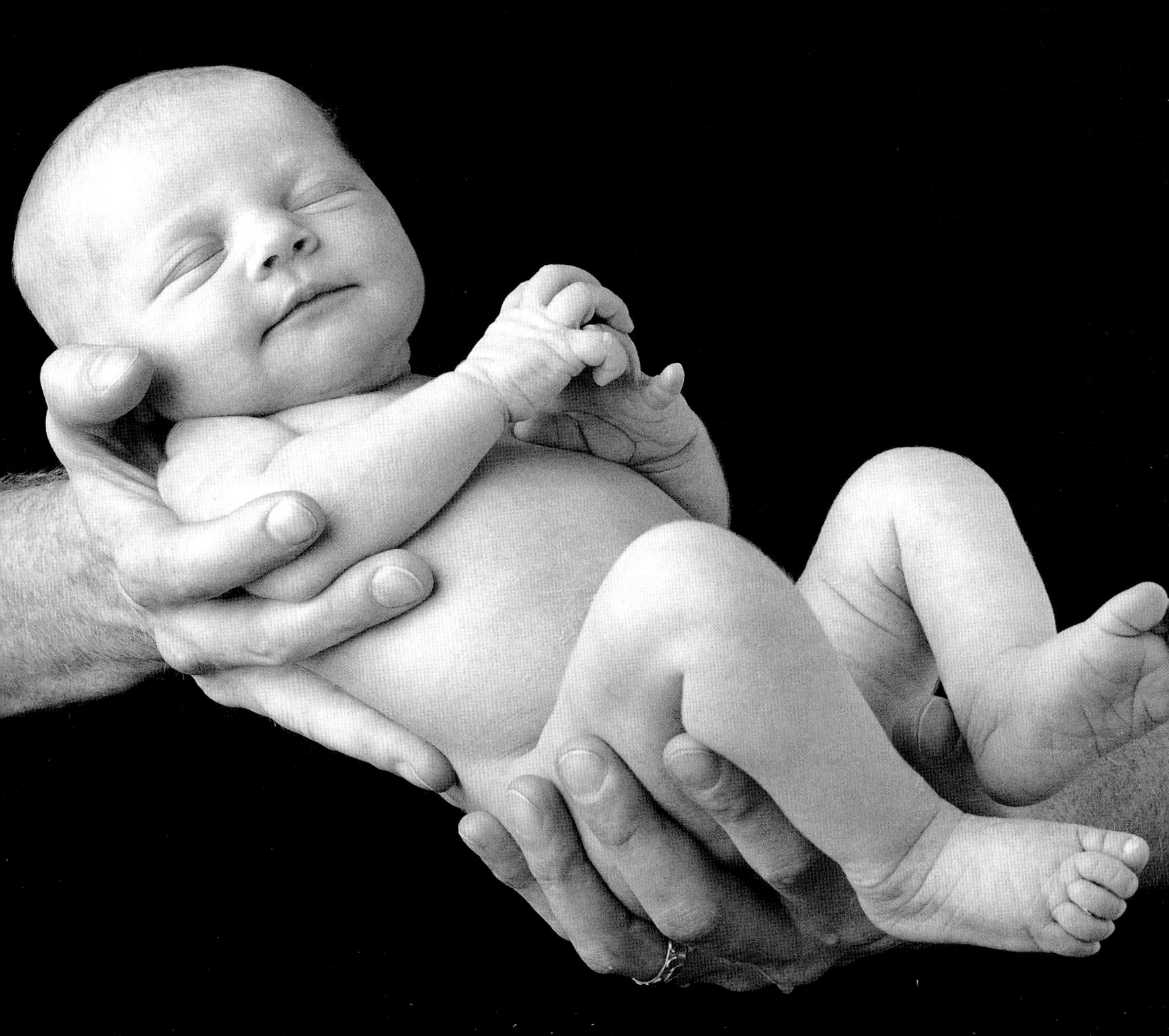

Hannah 6 days

21

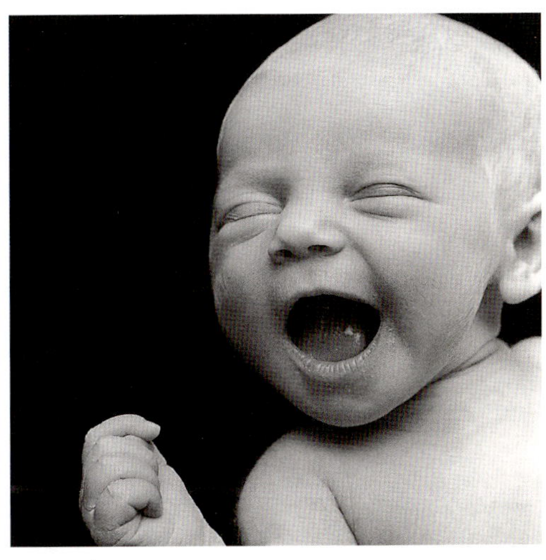

13 days

Dylan

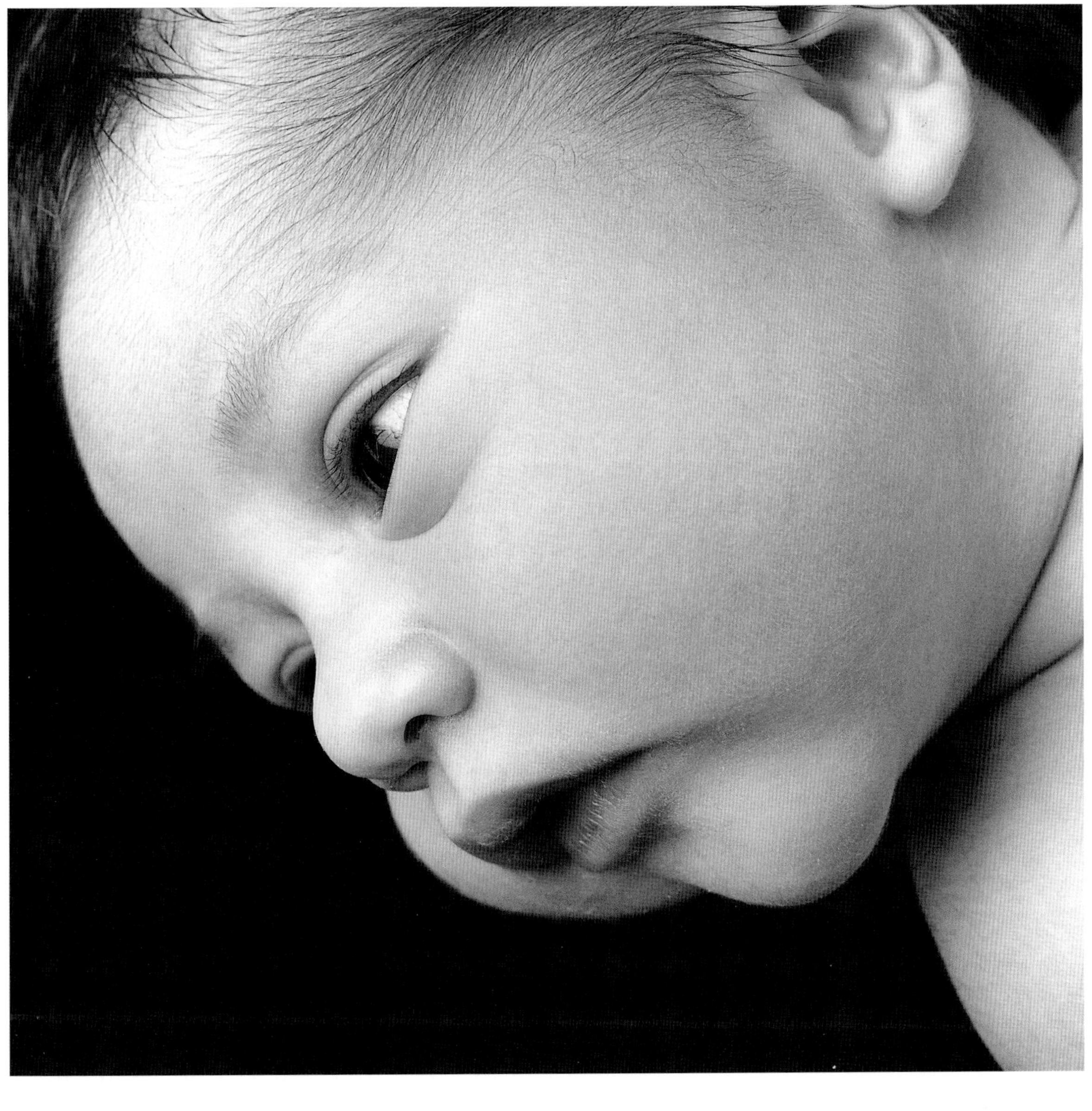

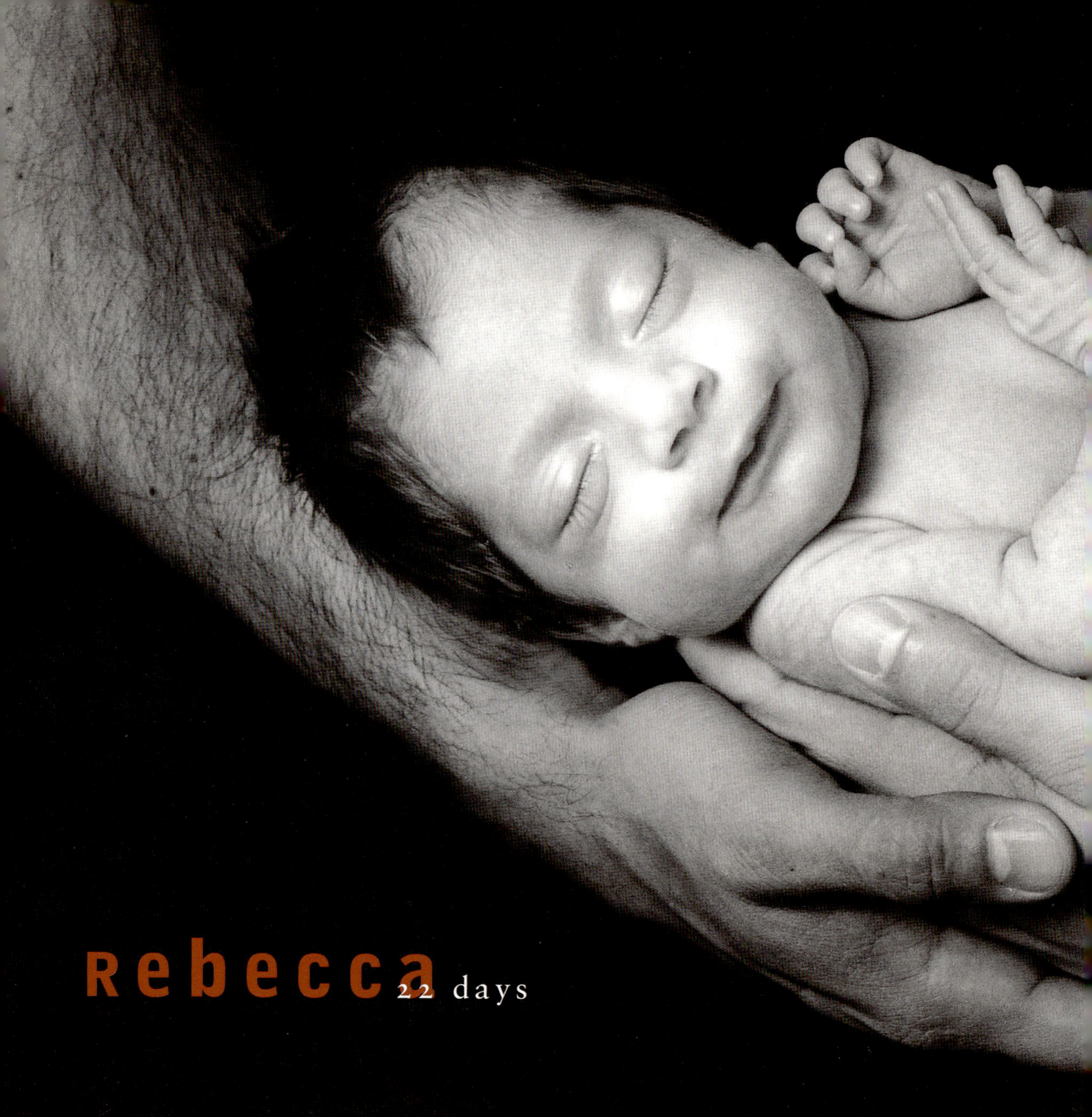
Rebecca 22 days

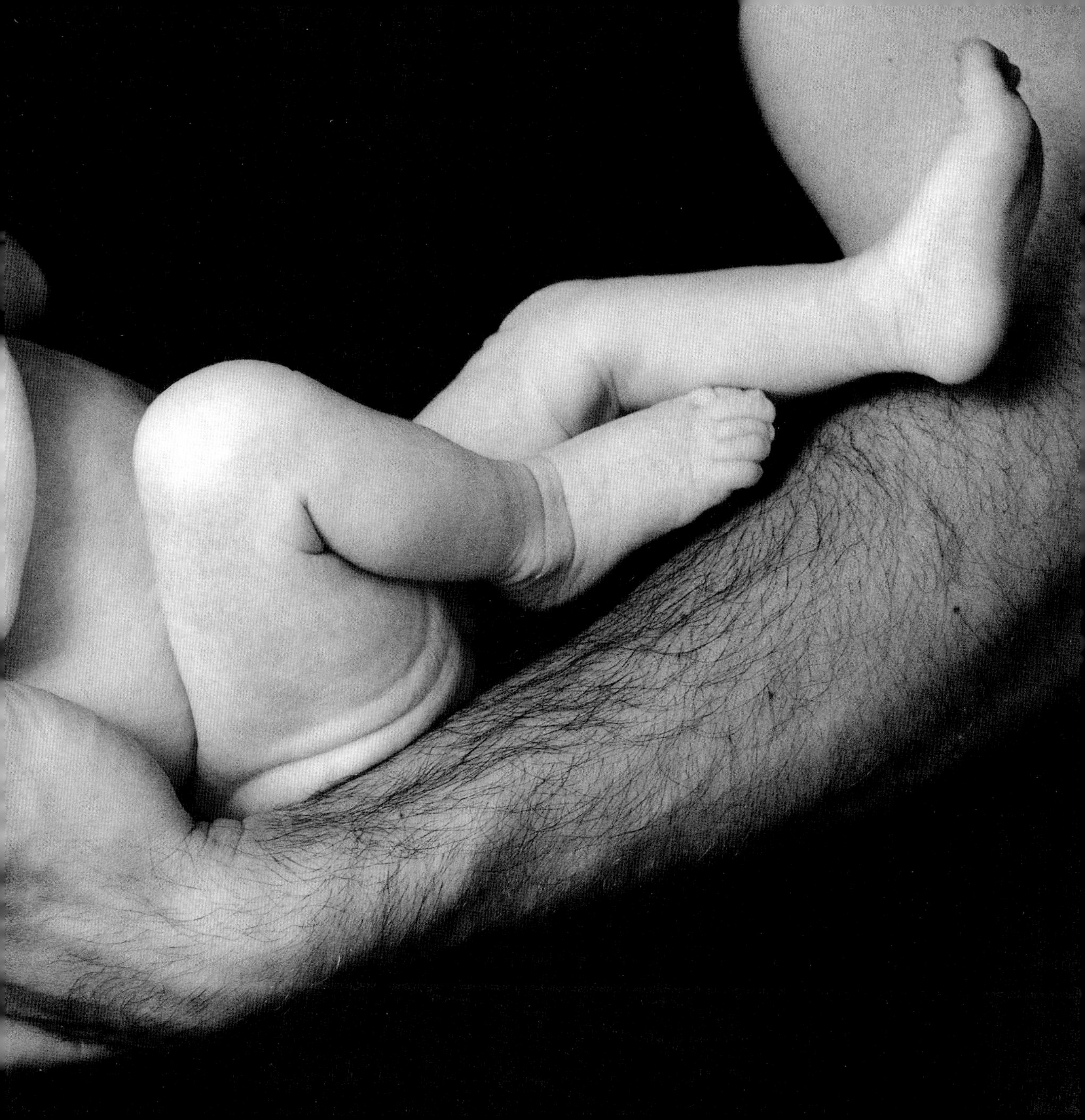

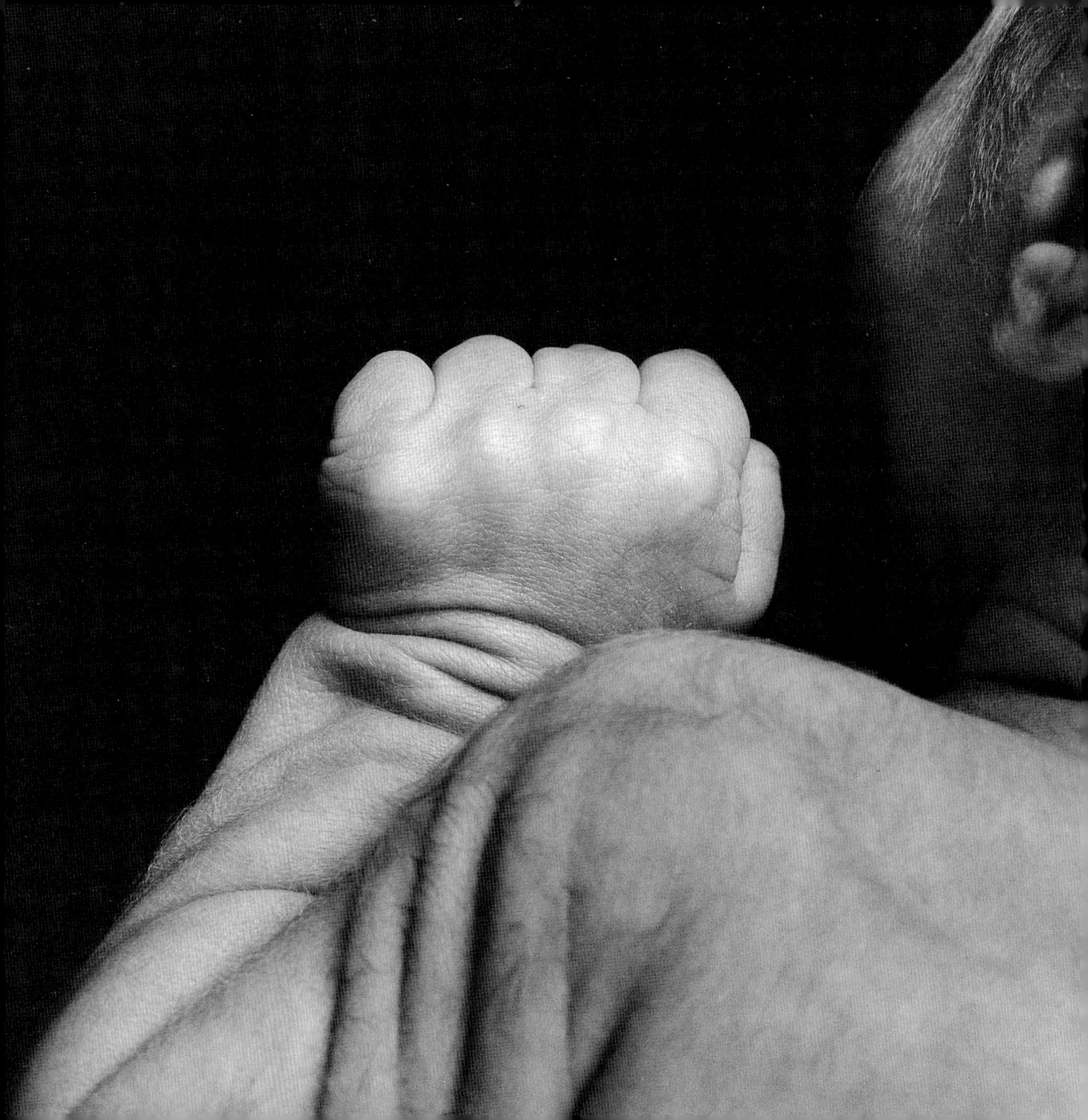

Tyler 9 days

Juliette 1 day

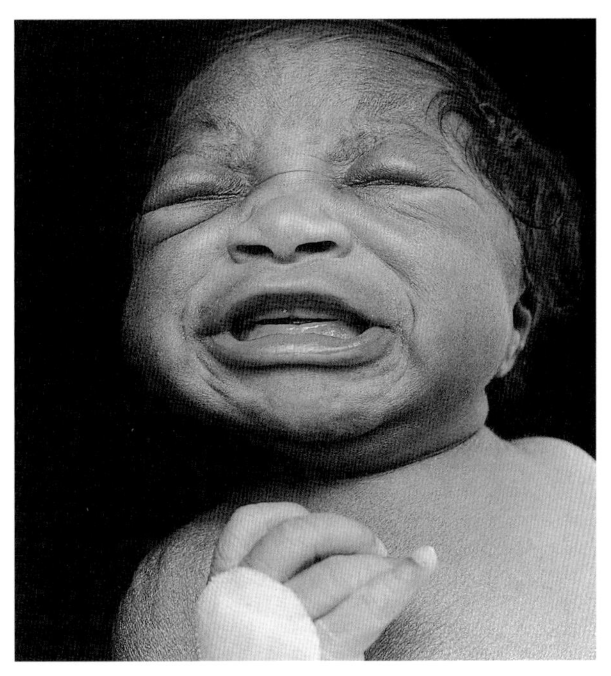

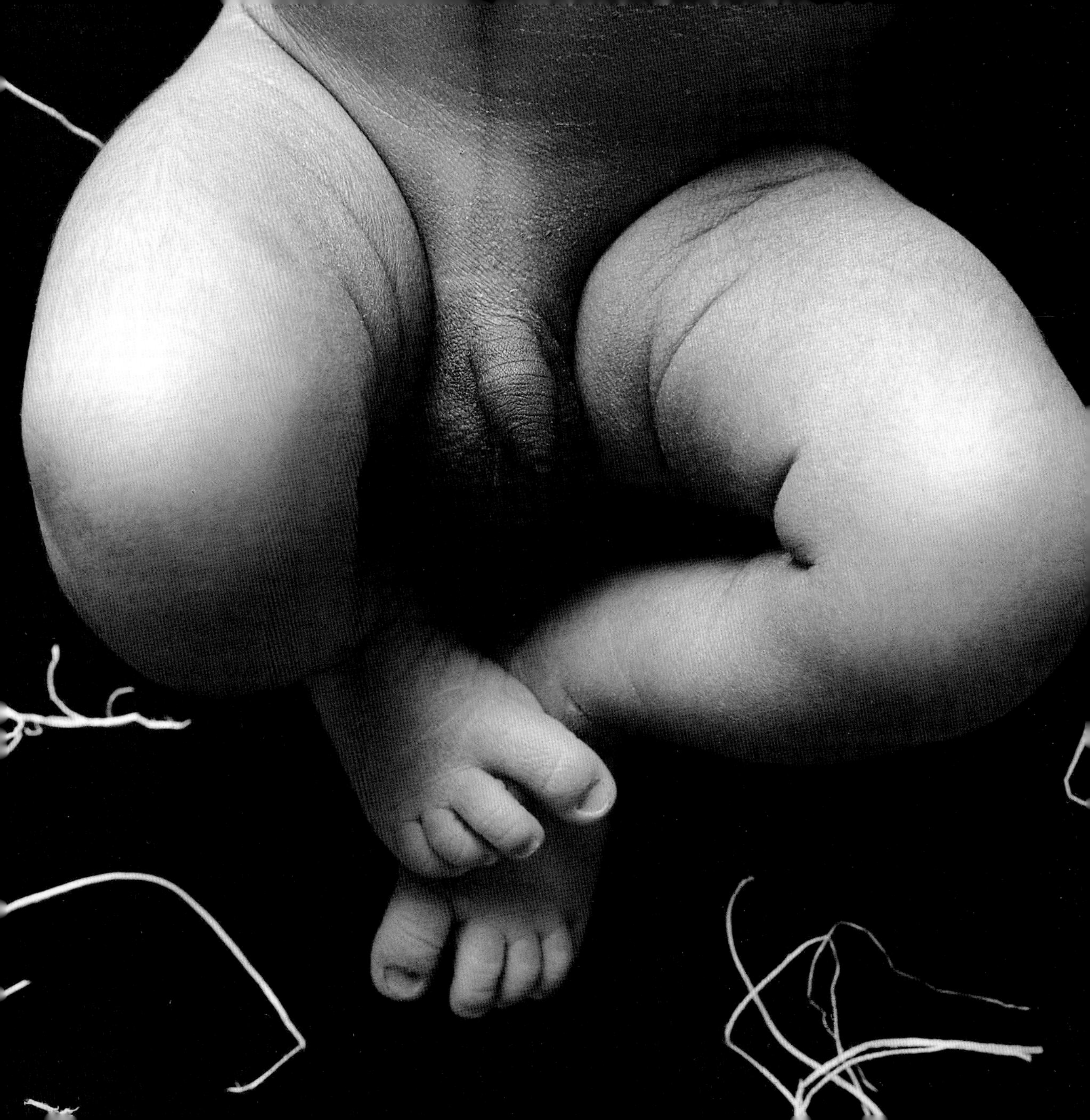

31

Tony

1 day

32

Ernst 12 days

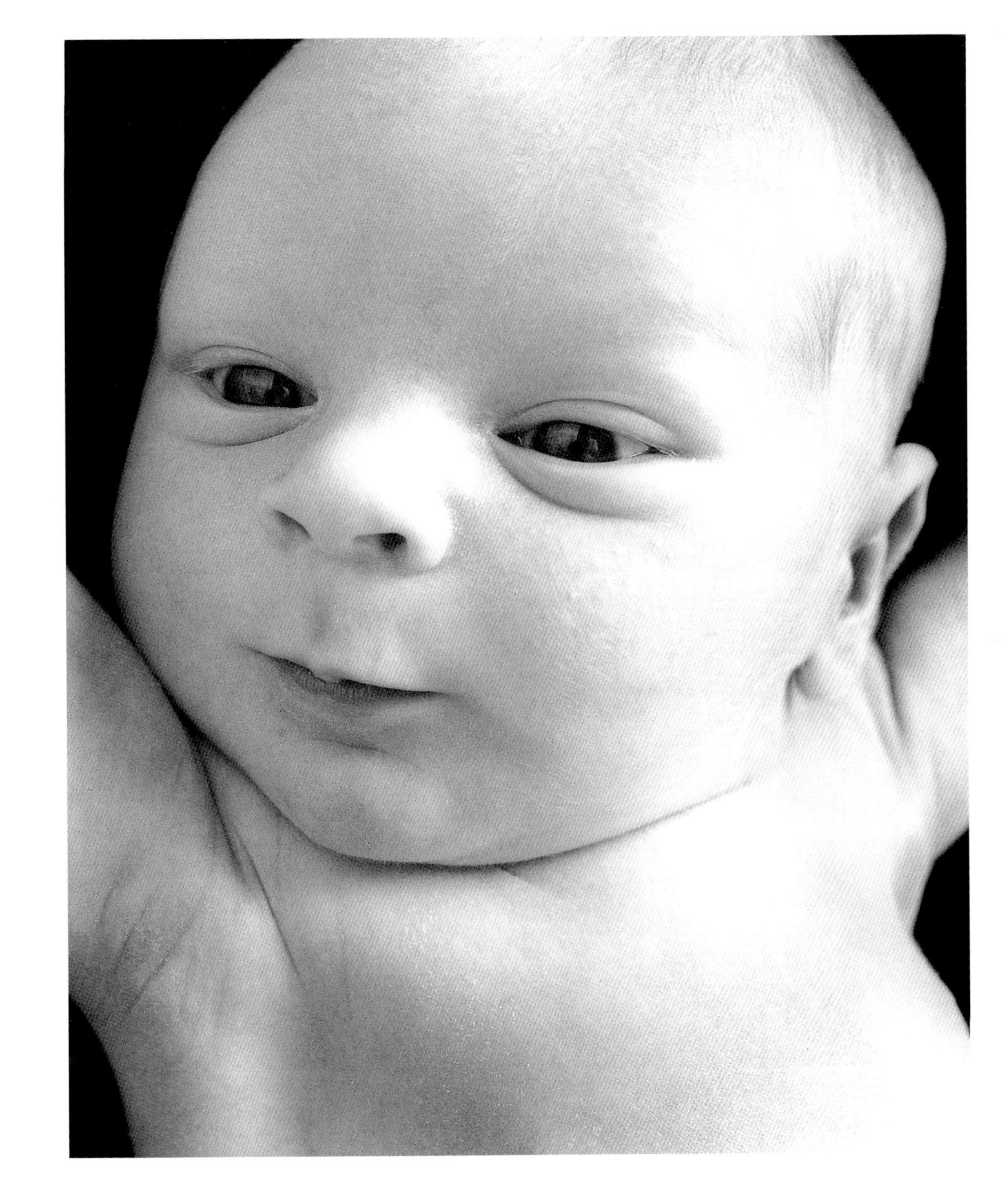

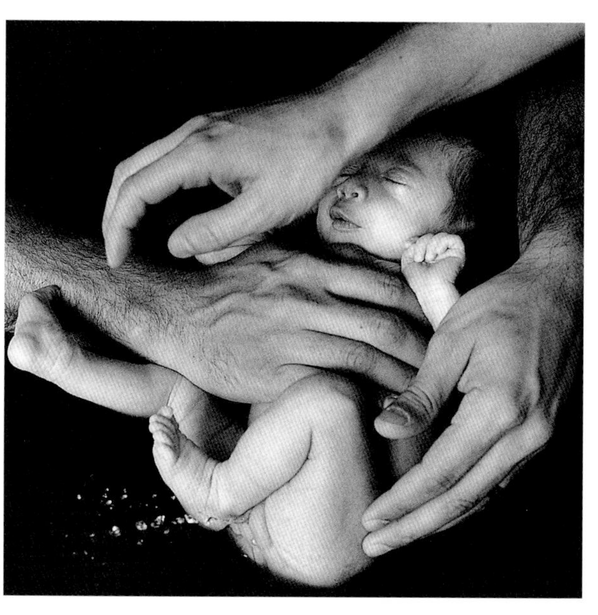

rebecca 22 days

36

3 days **vanessa**

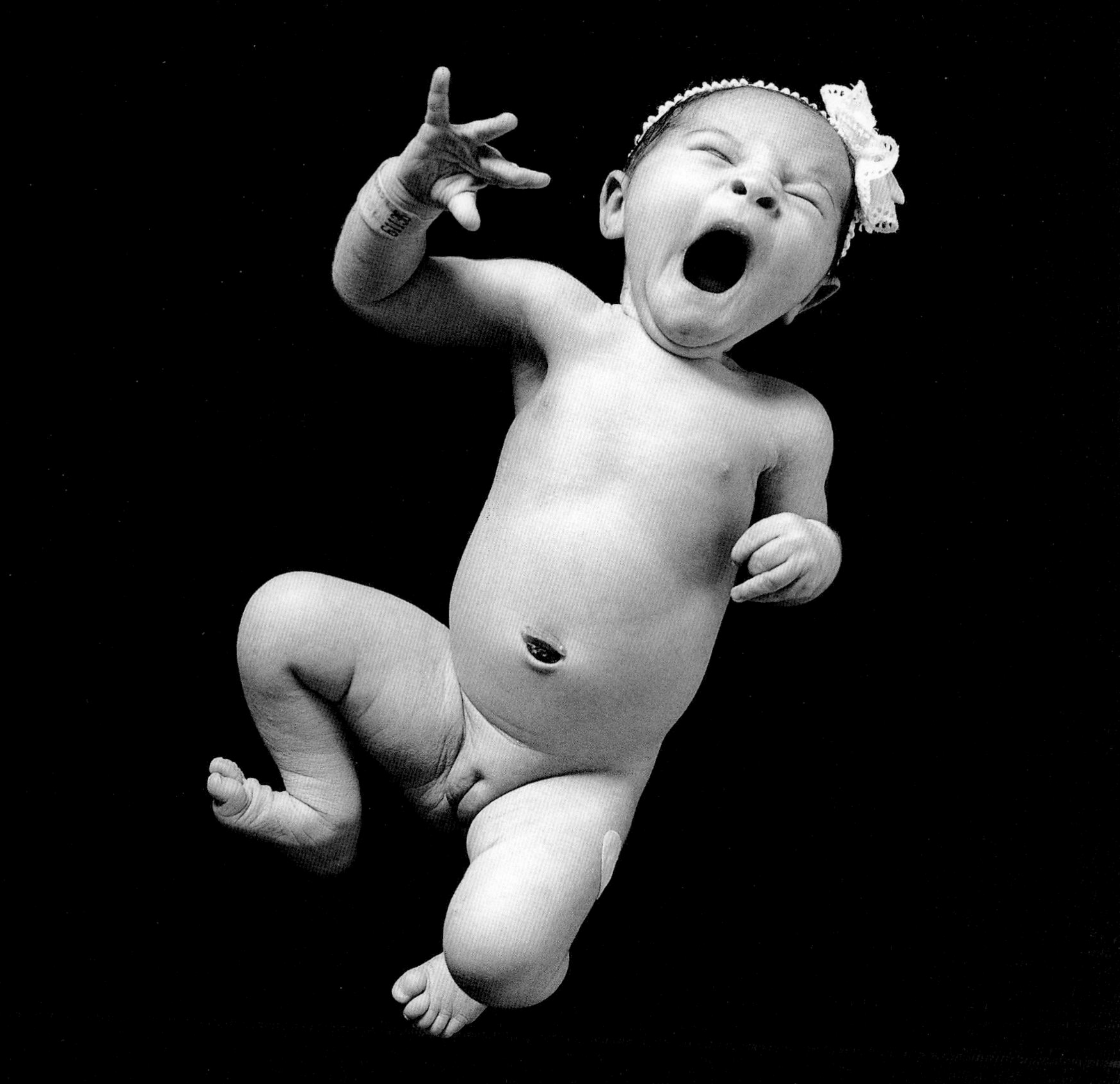

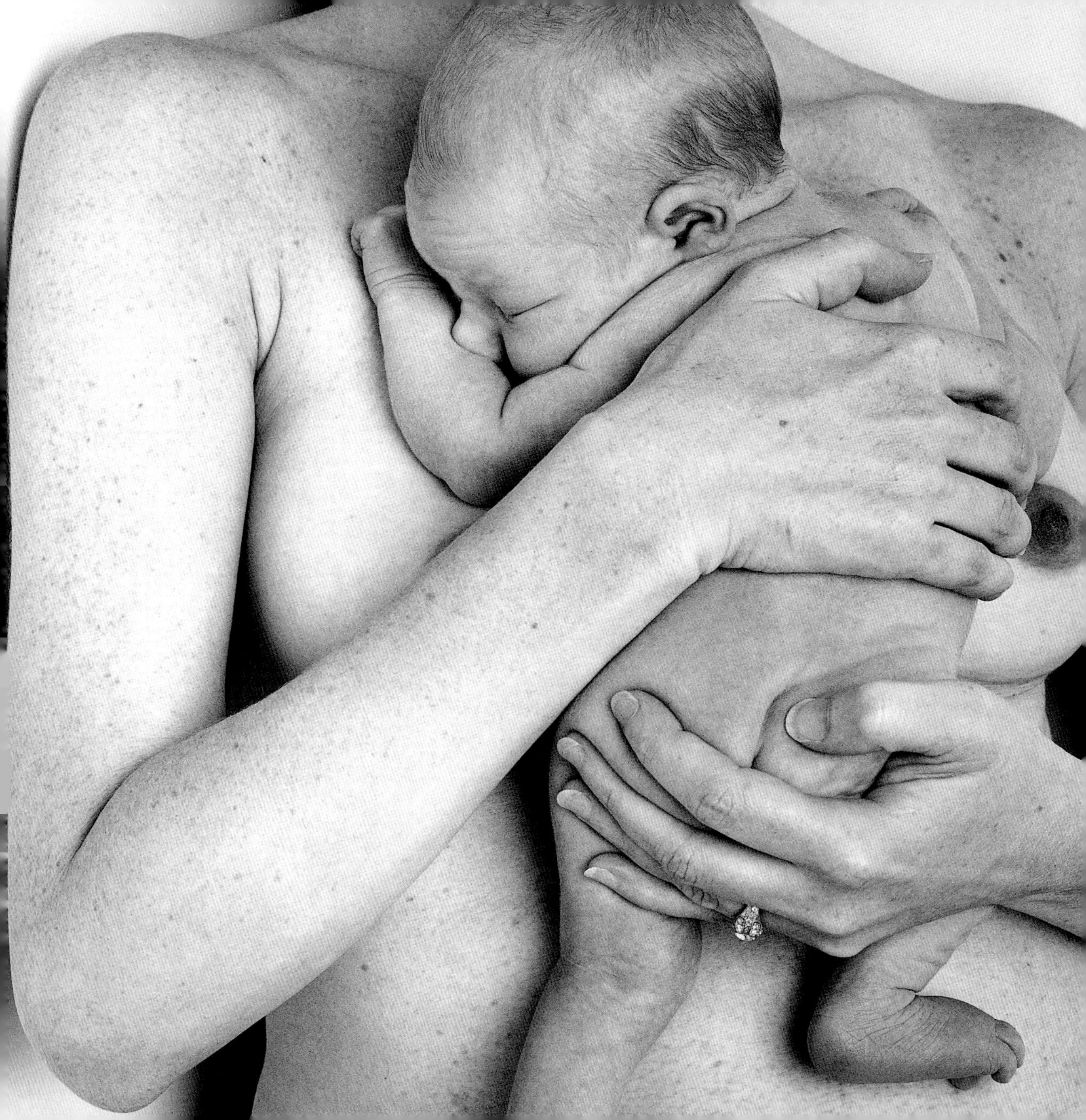

mackenzie 3 days

4 days

caira

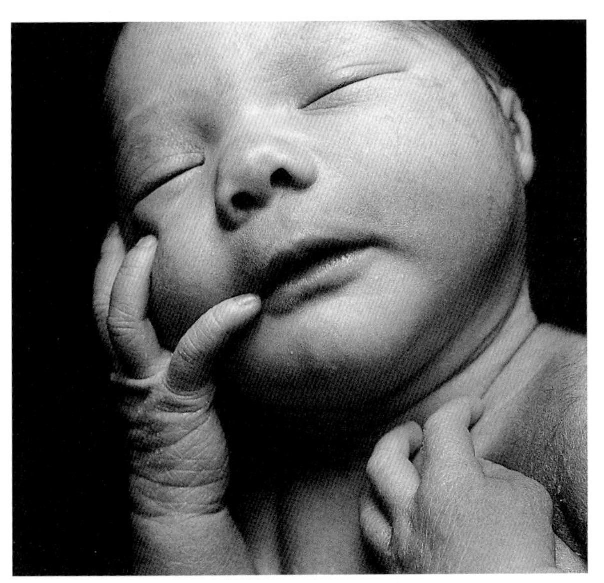

julia 9 days

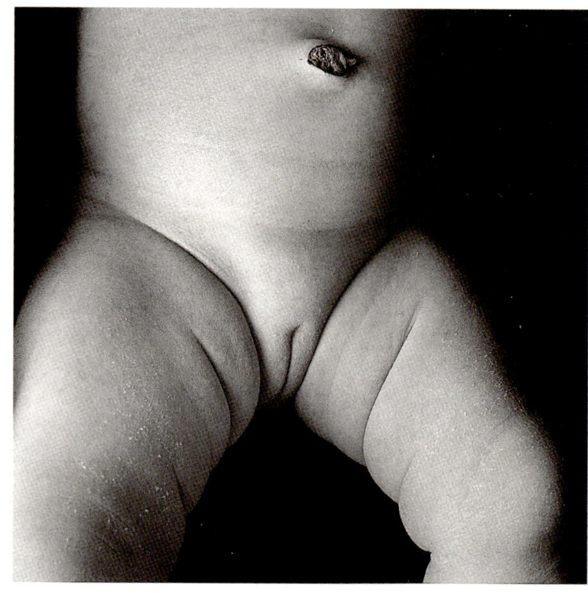

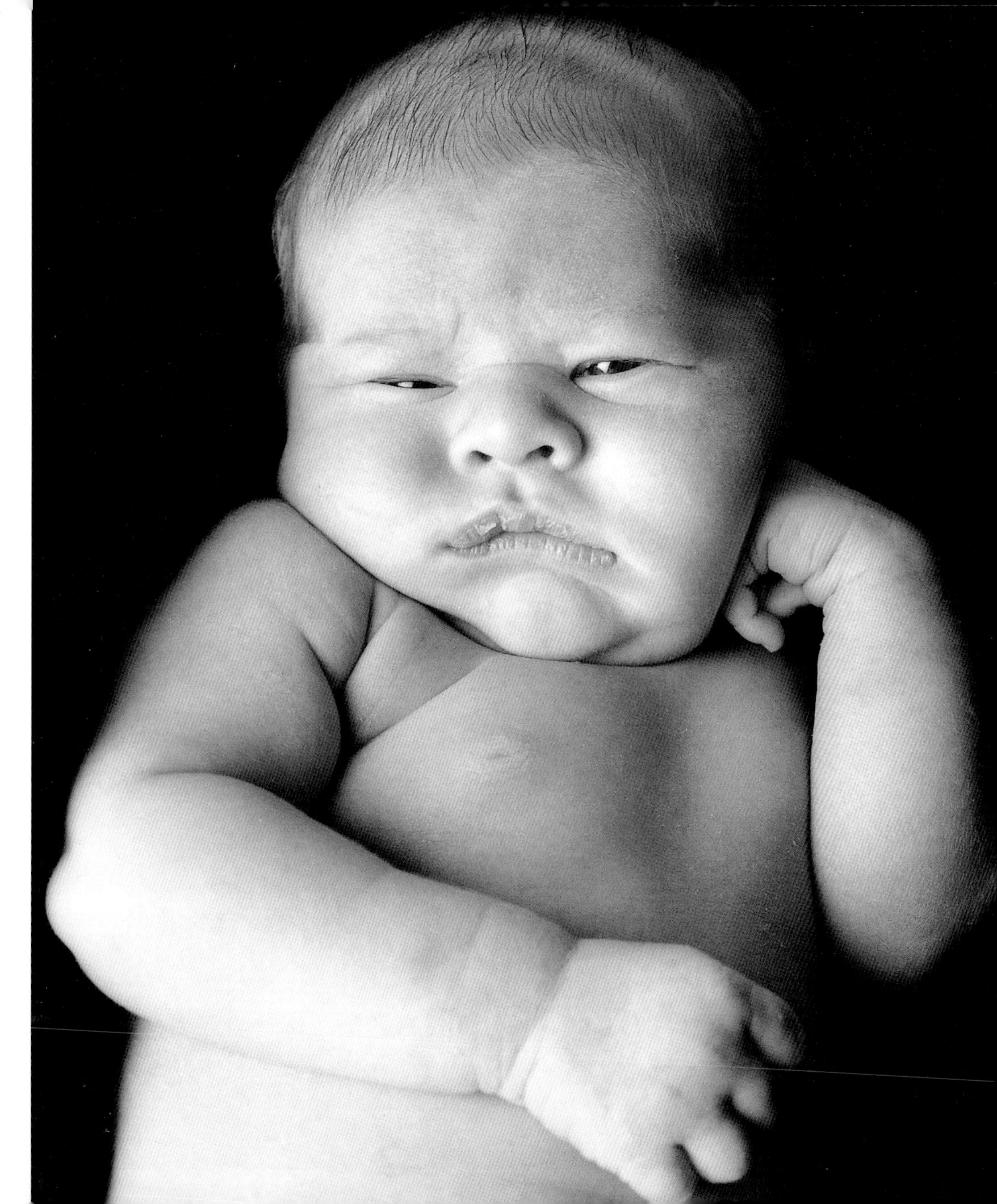

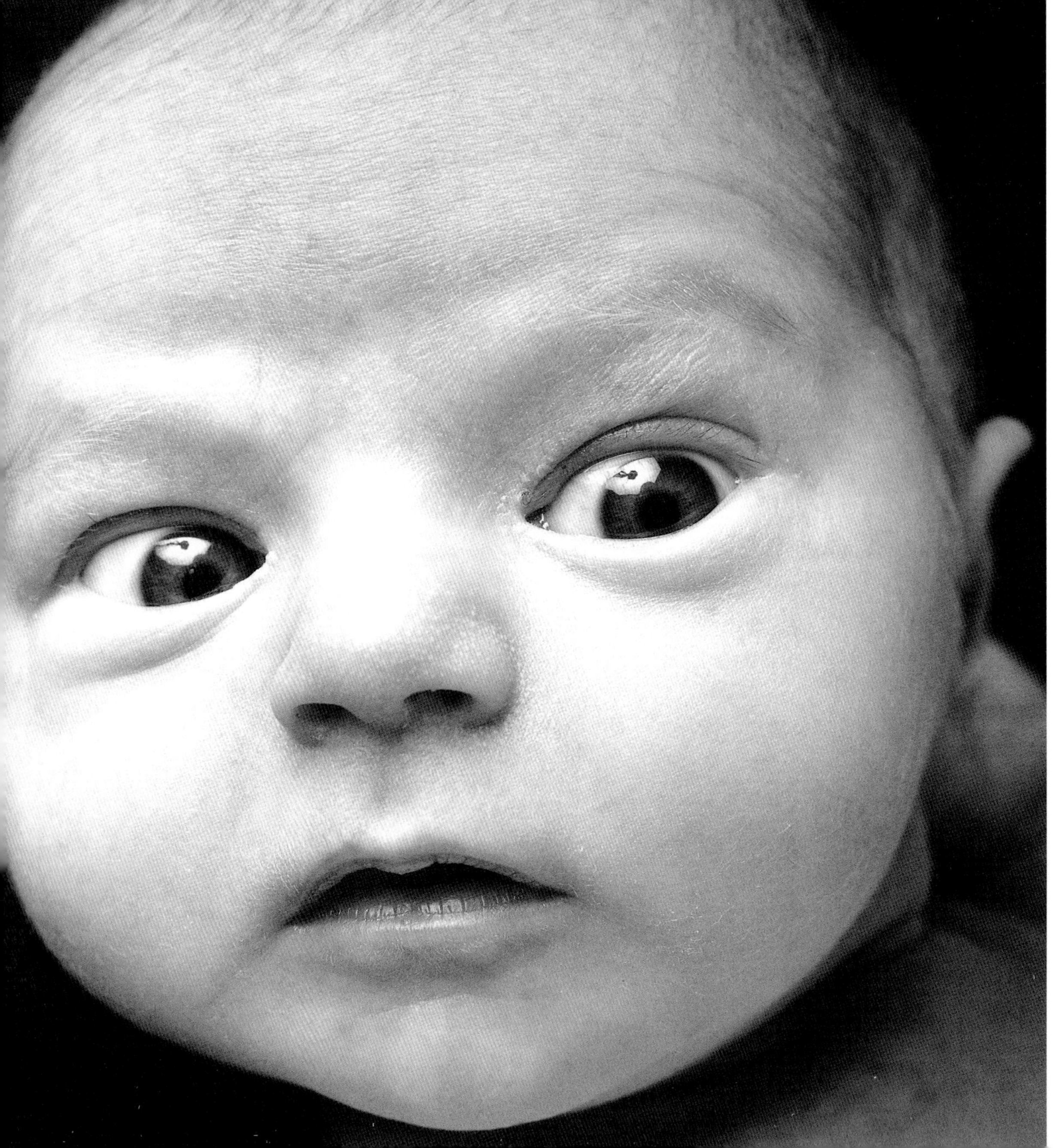

7 days Amy

46

Daniel 13 days

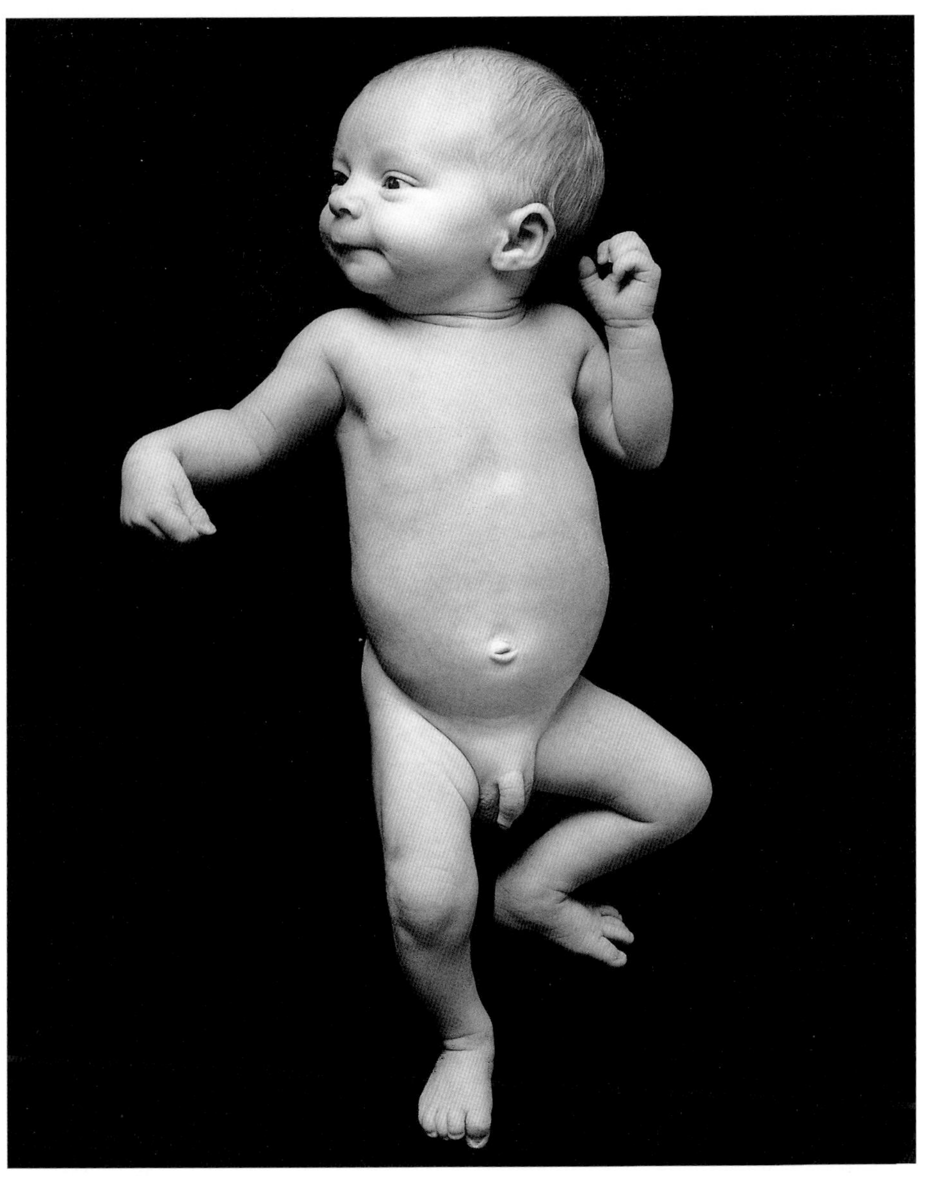

sophia 10 days

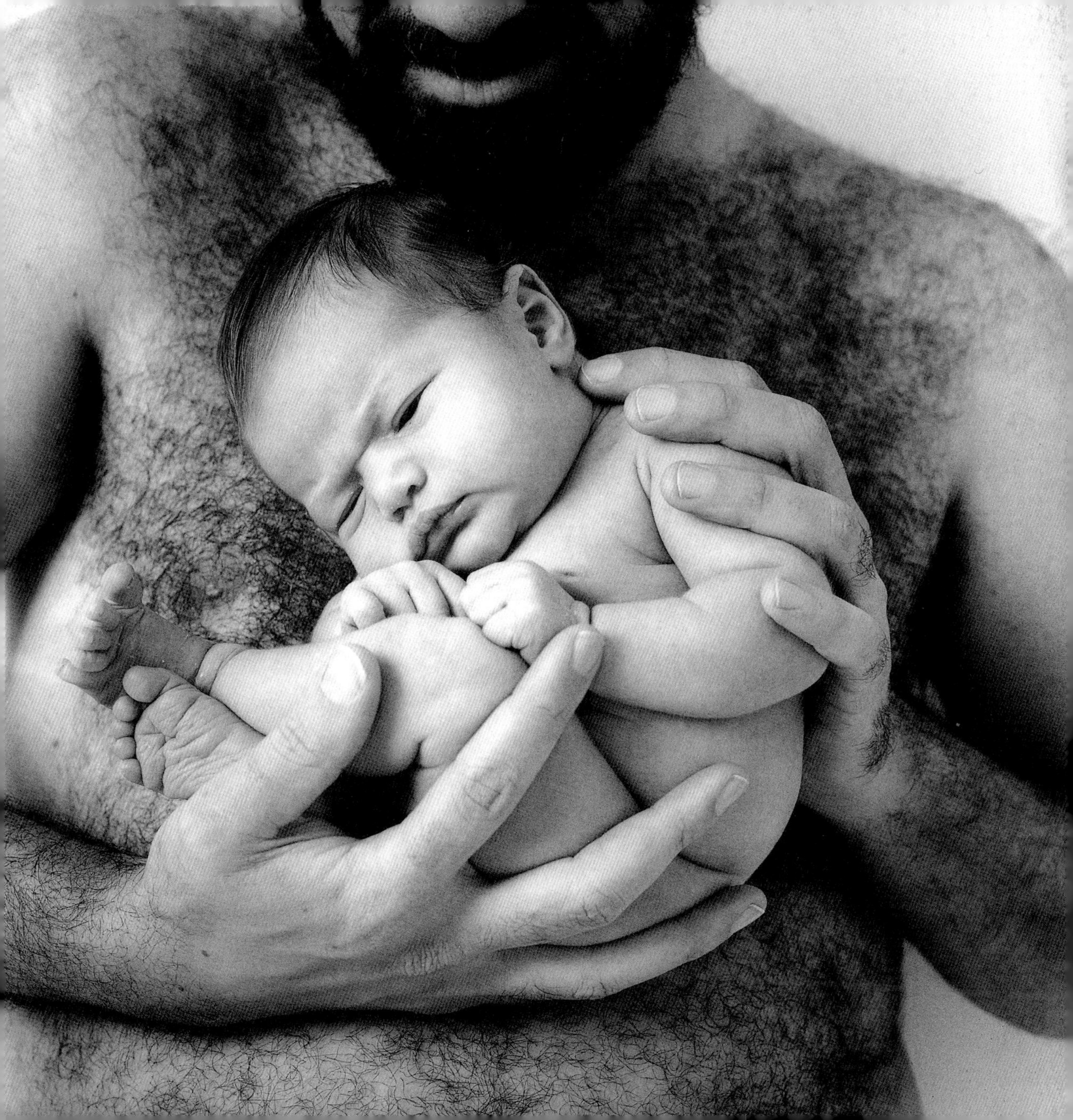

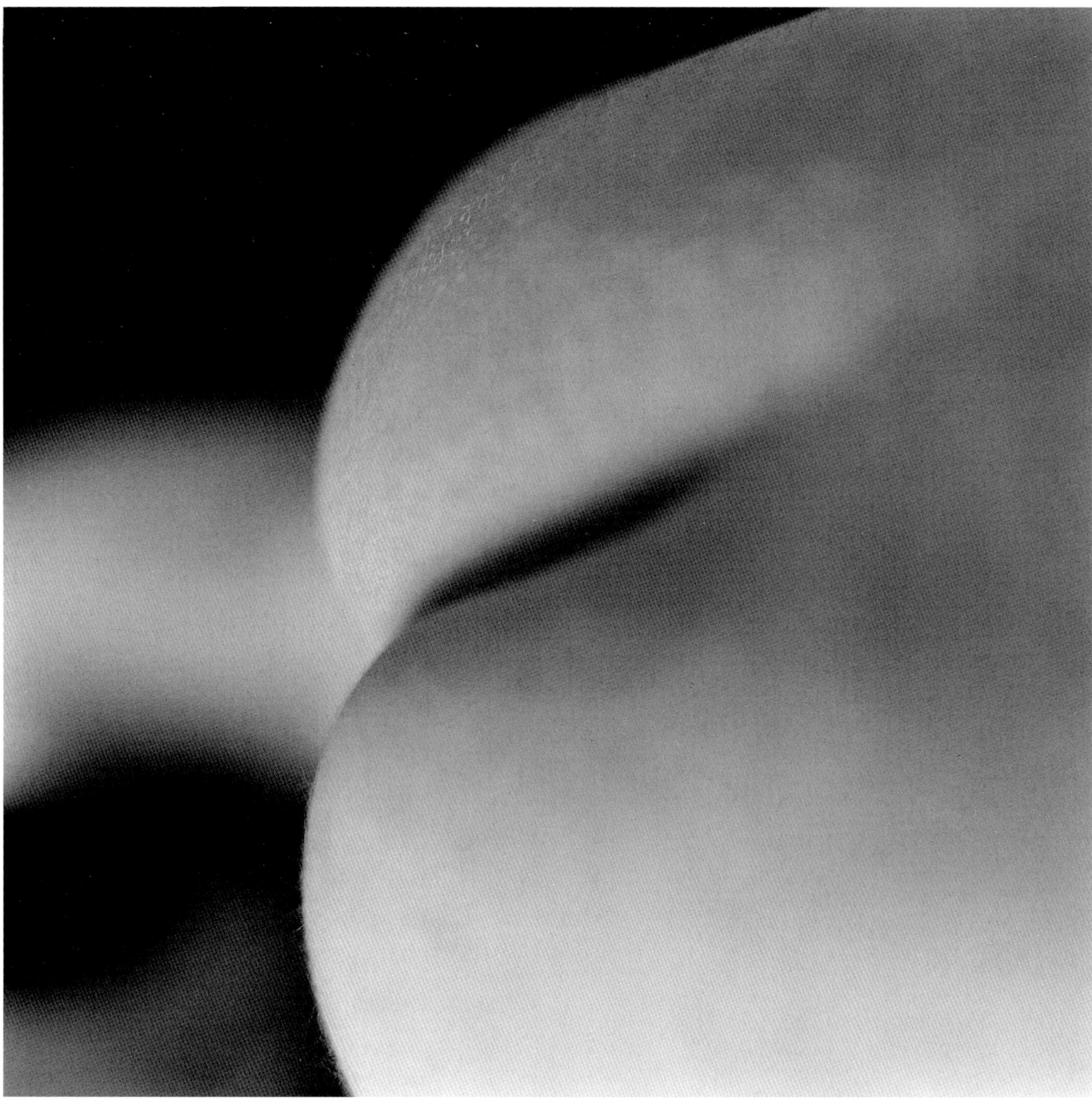

Hannah Rose

5 days

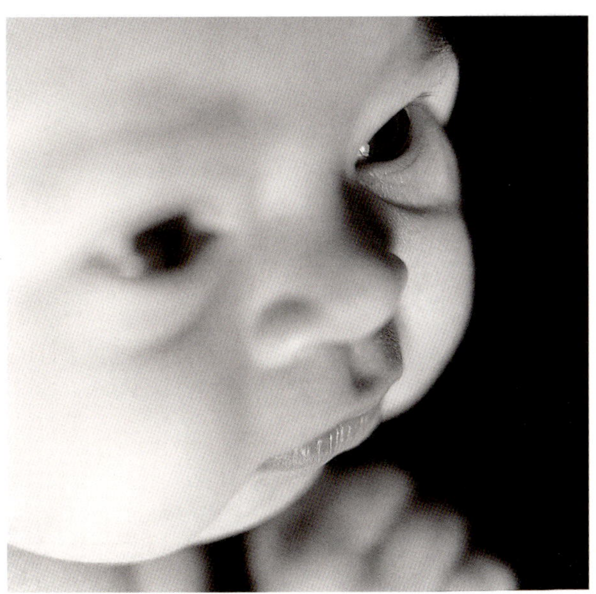

Jenna and Devan

4 days

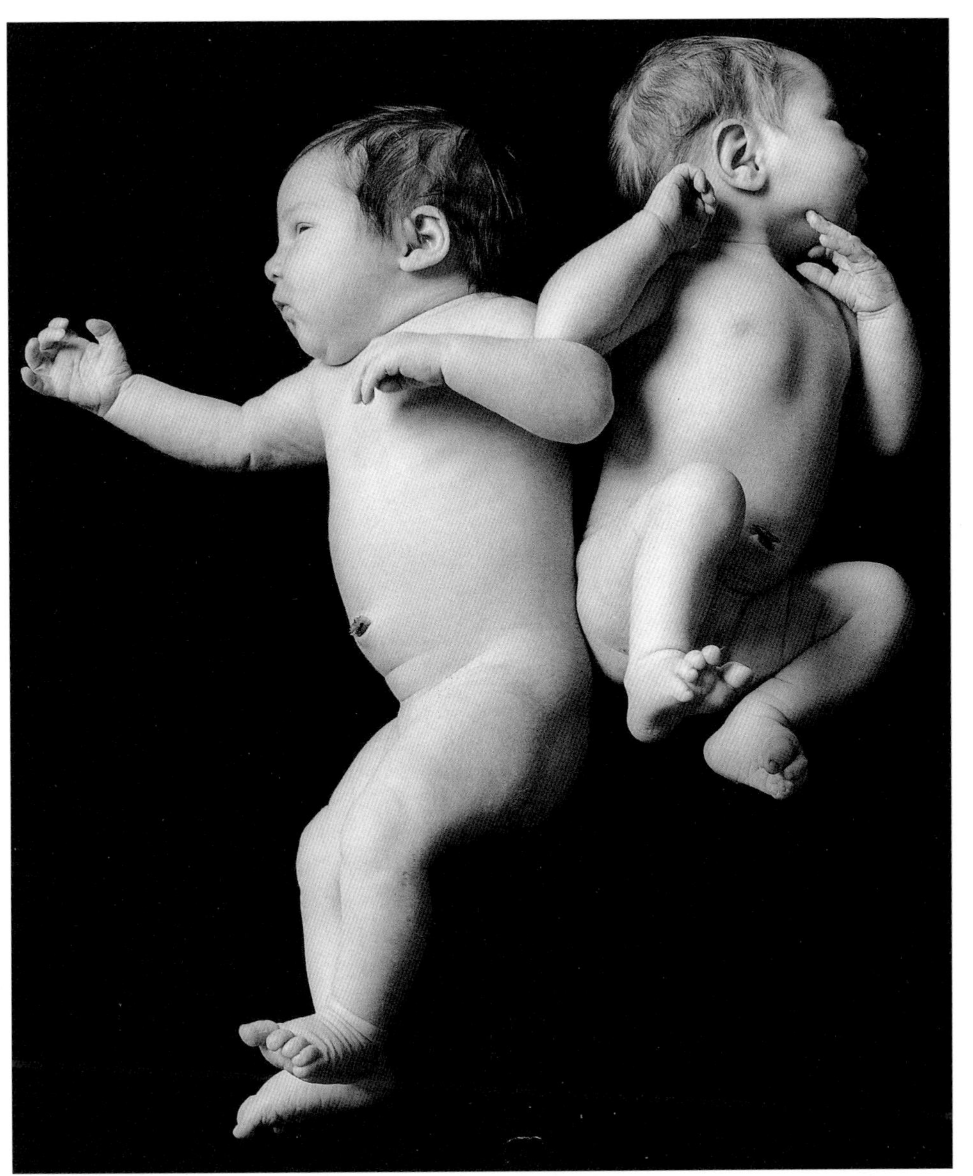

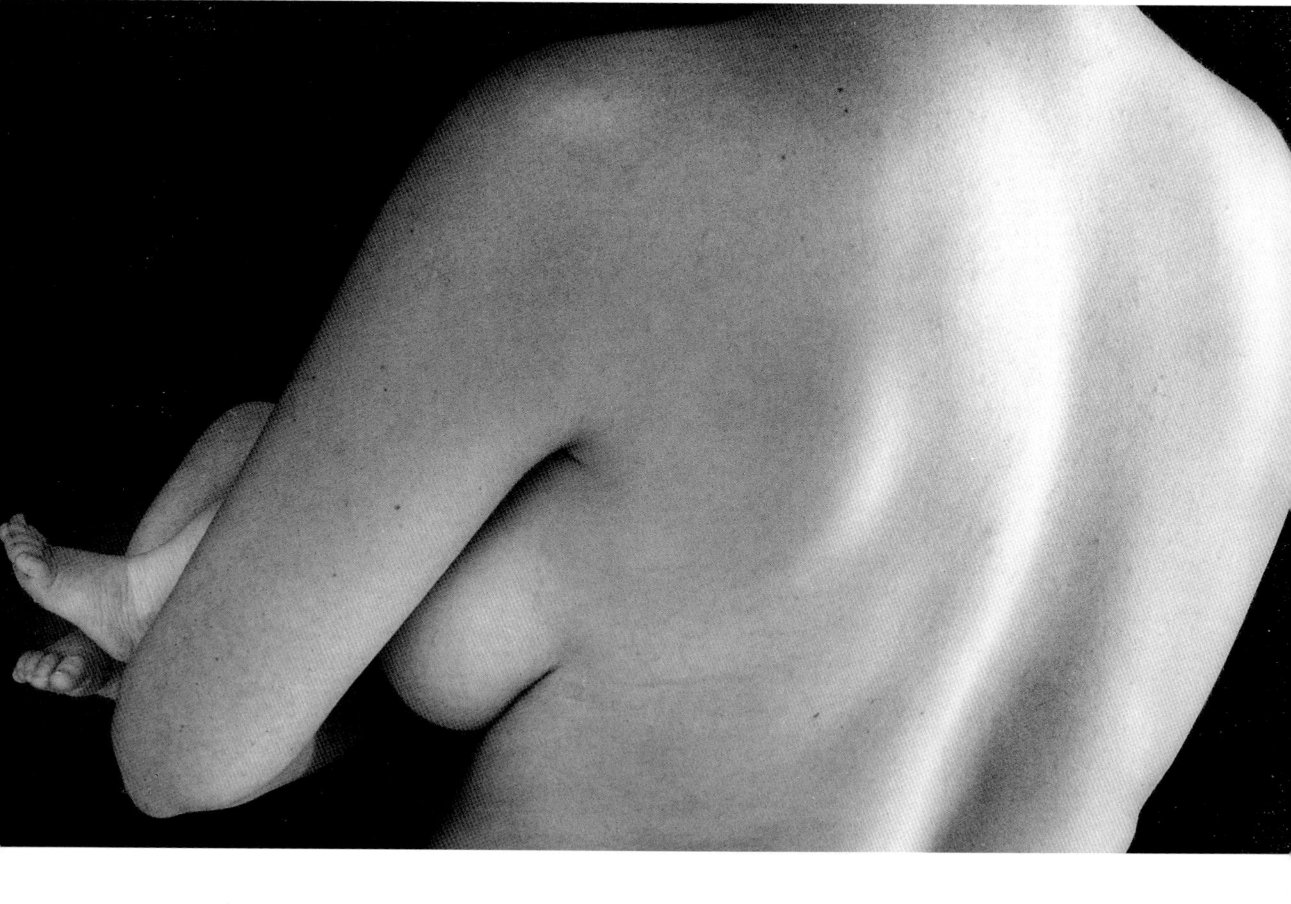

mekiah

6 days

56

12 days

Evelyn

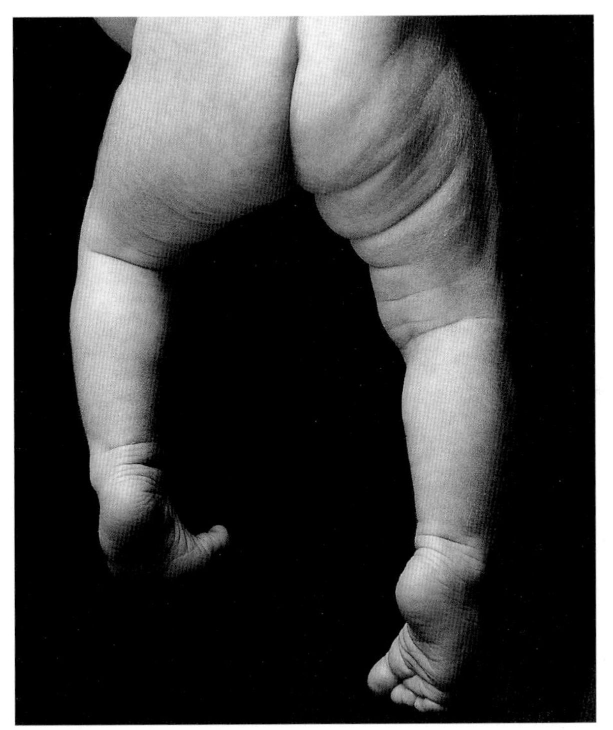

1 day celeste

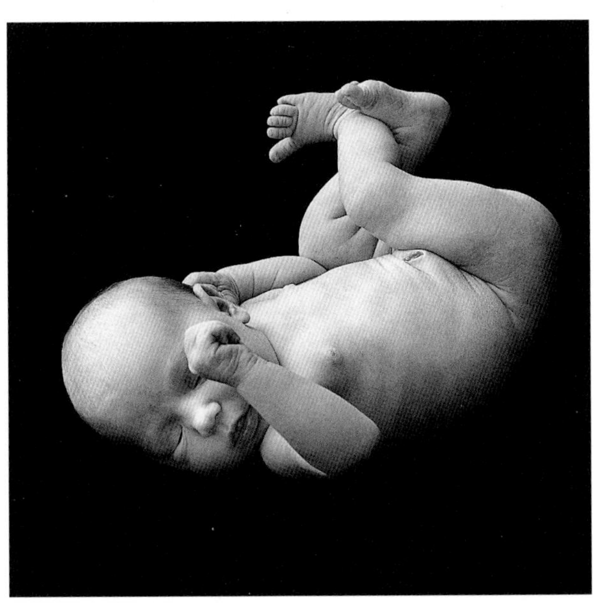

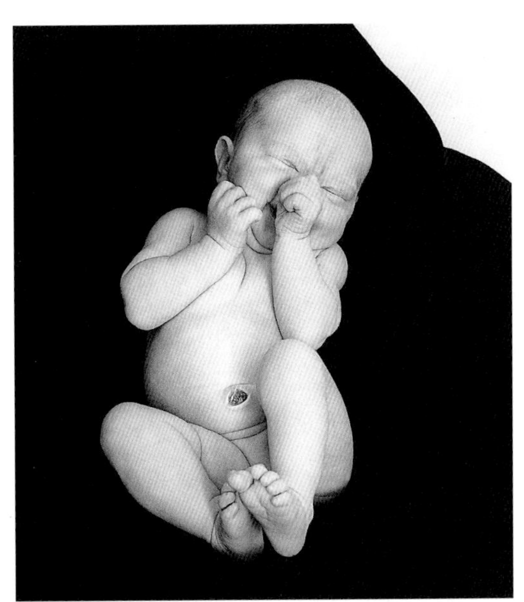

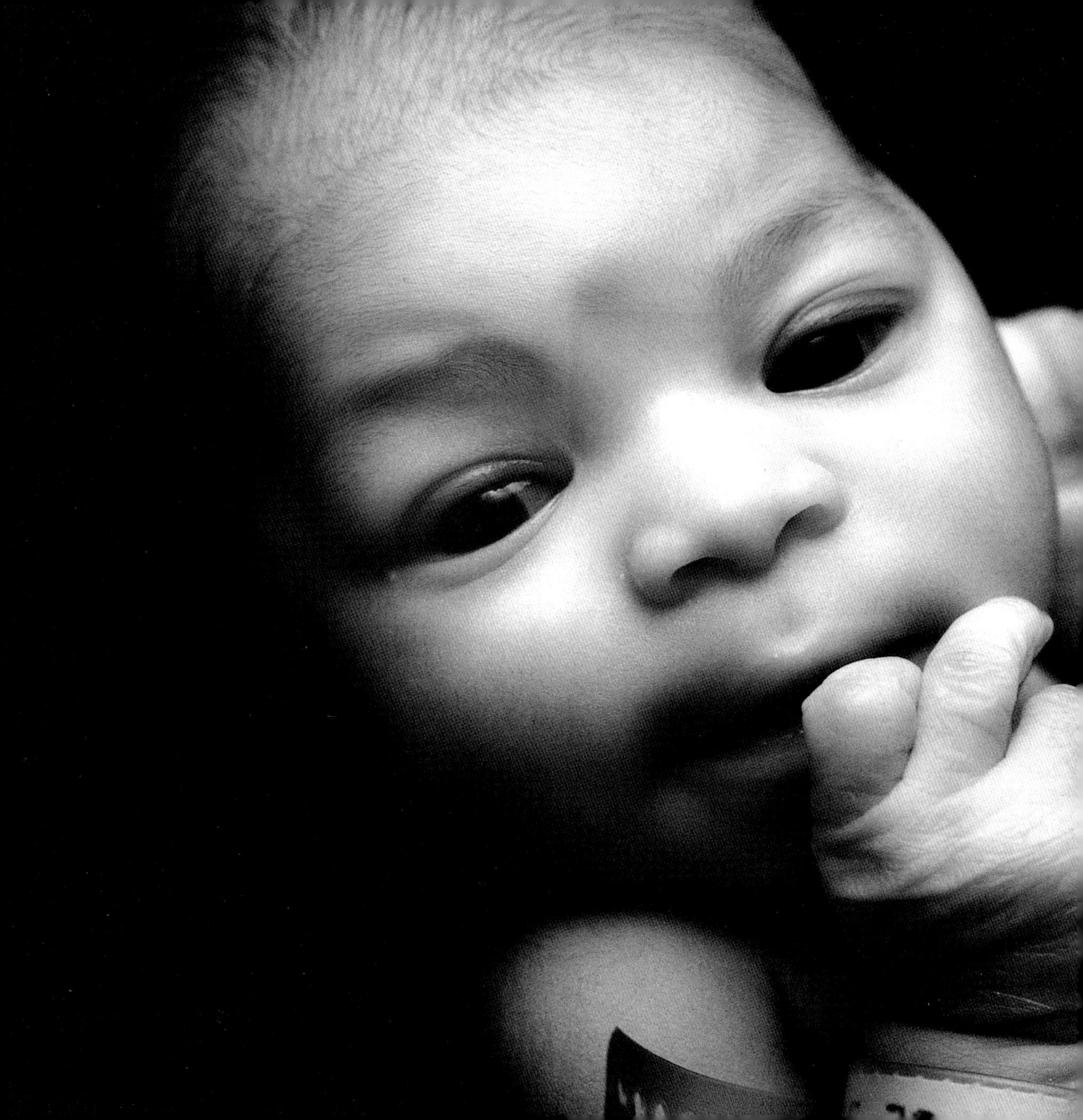

1 day **jasmine**

Amber

3 days

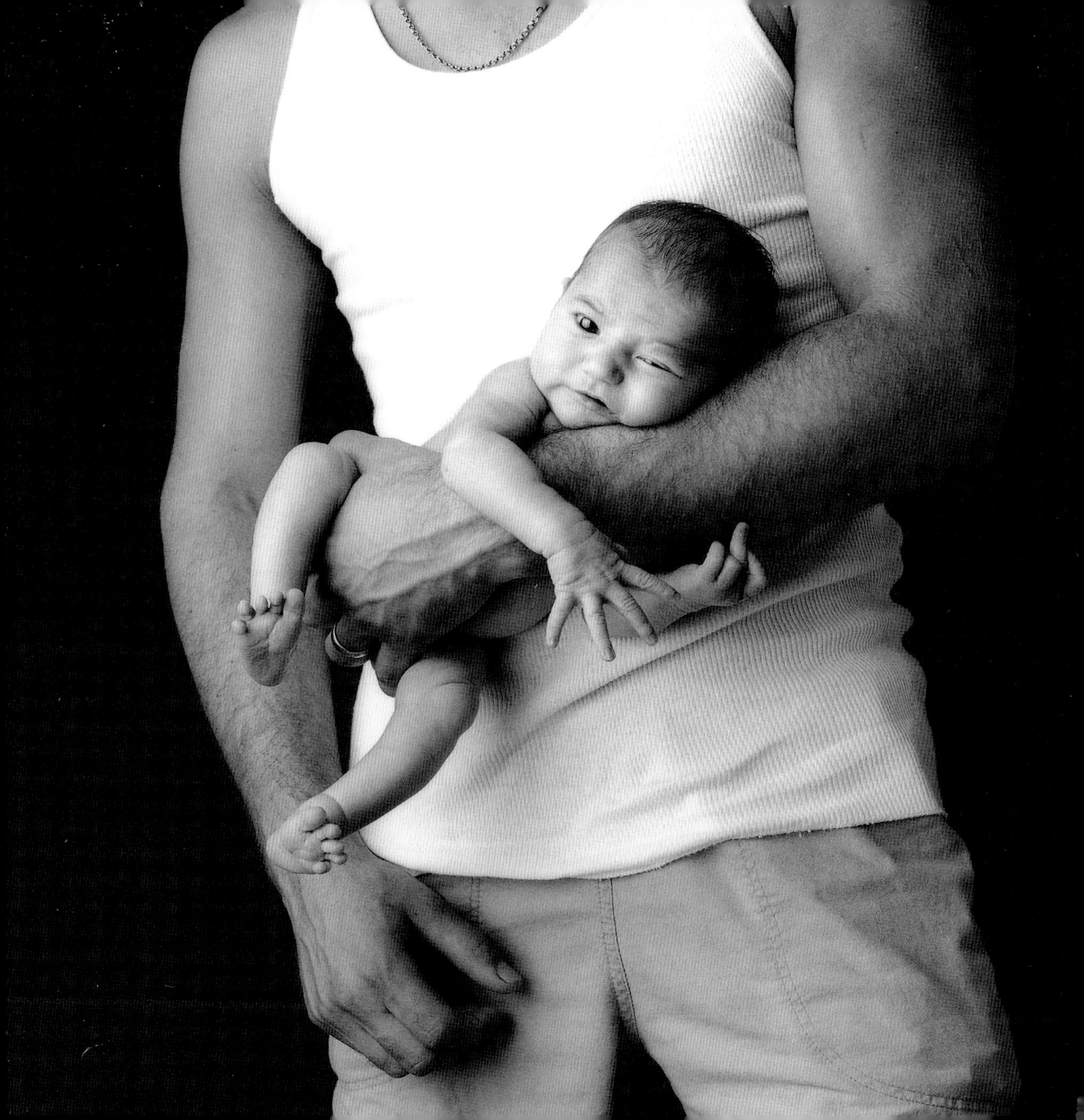

Noelani 9 days

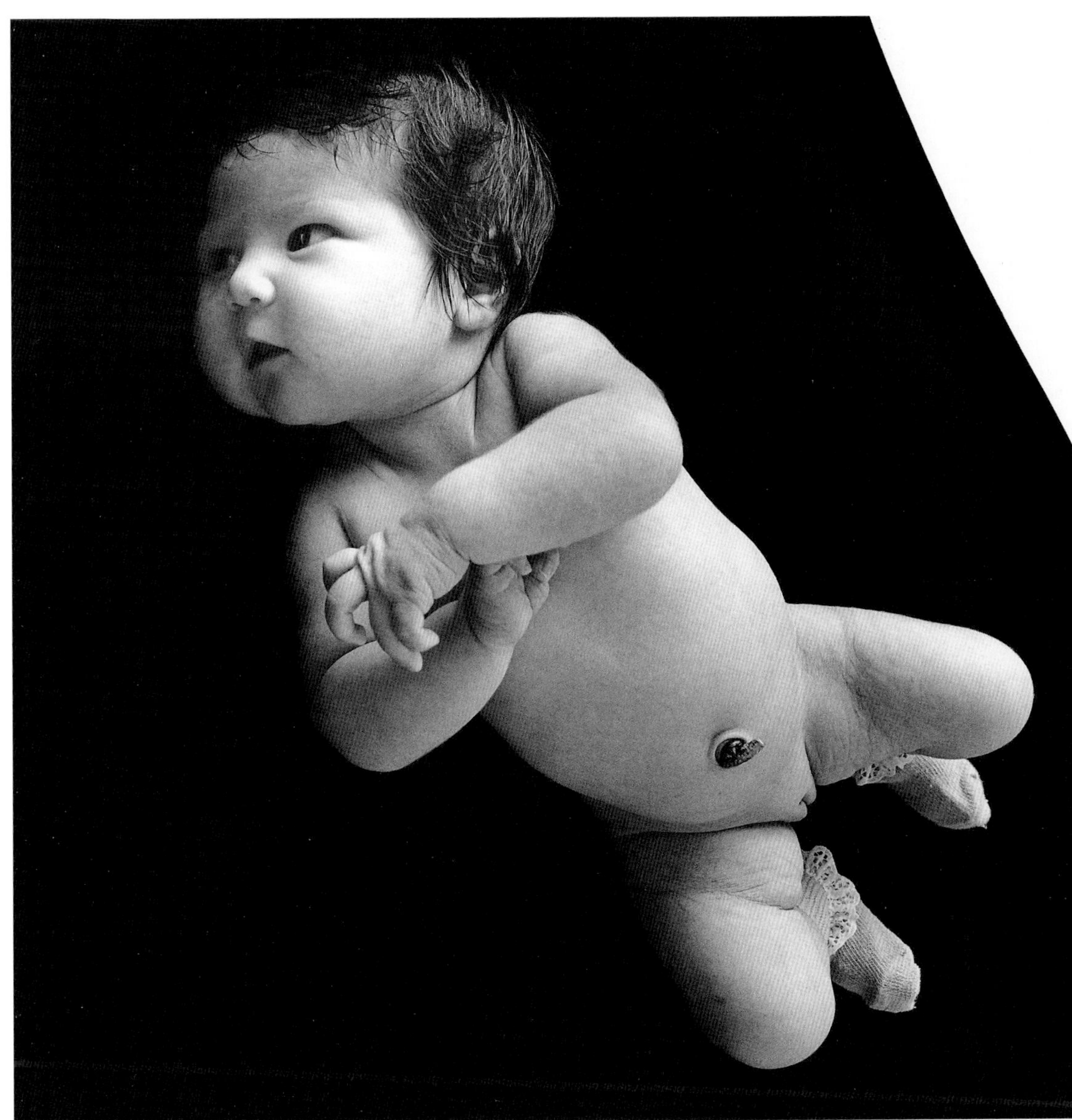

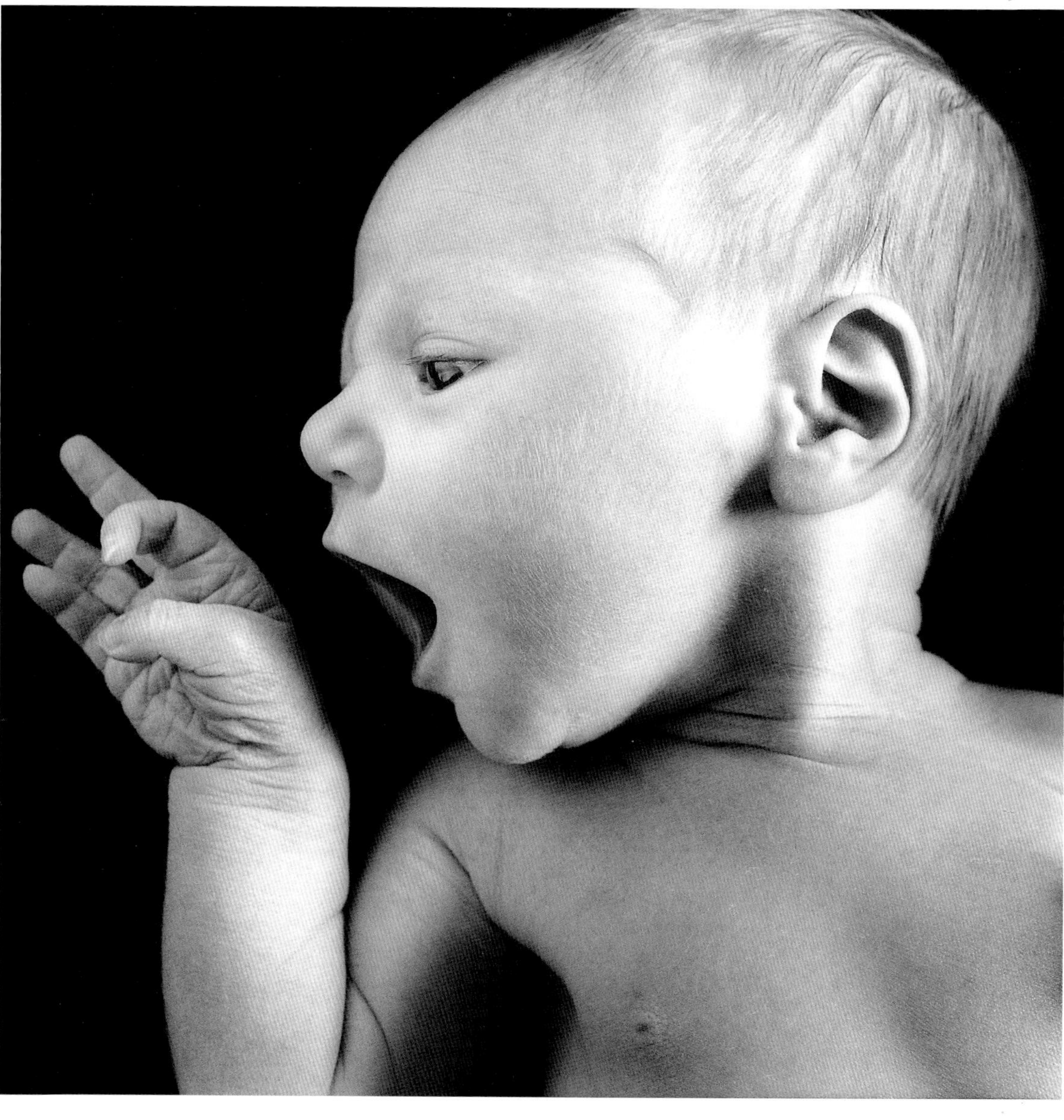

4 days

samantha

selena 4 days

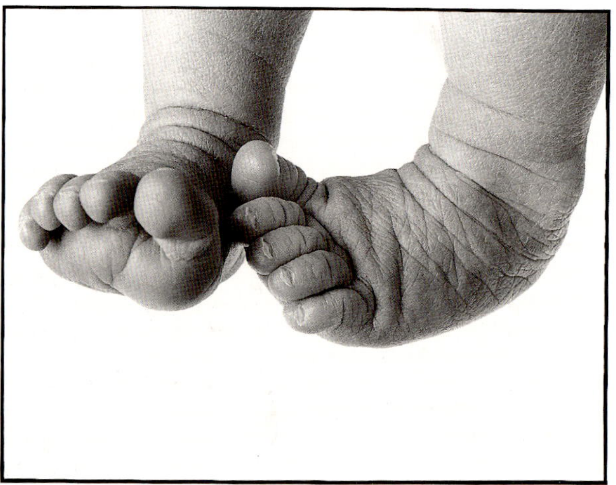

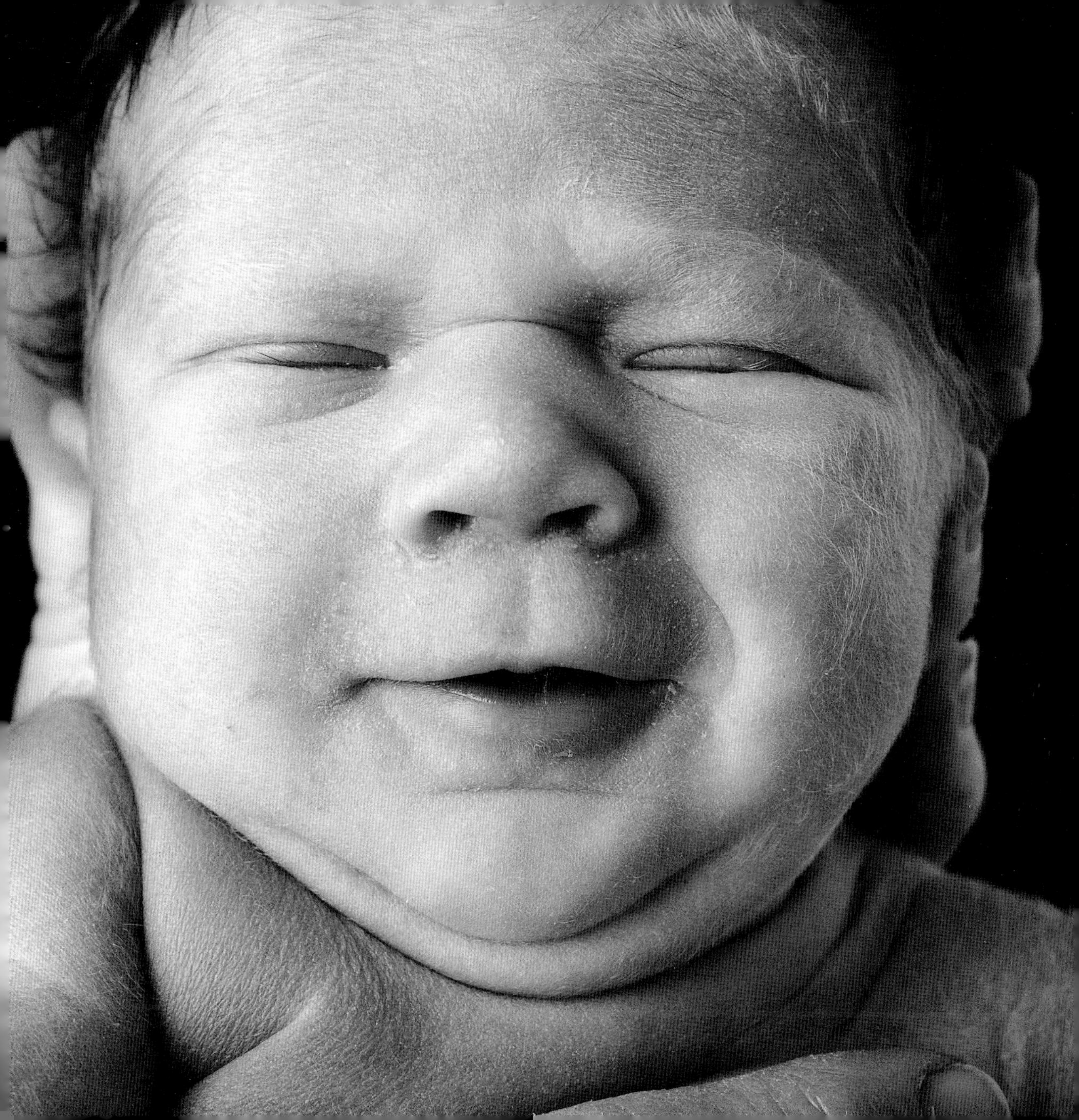

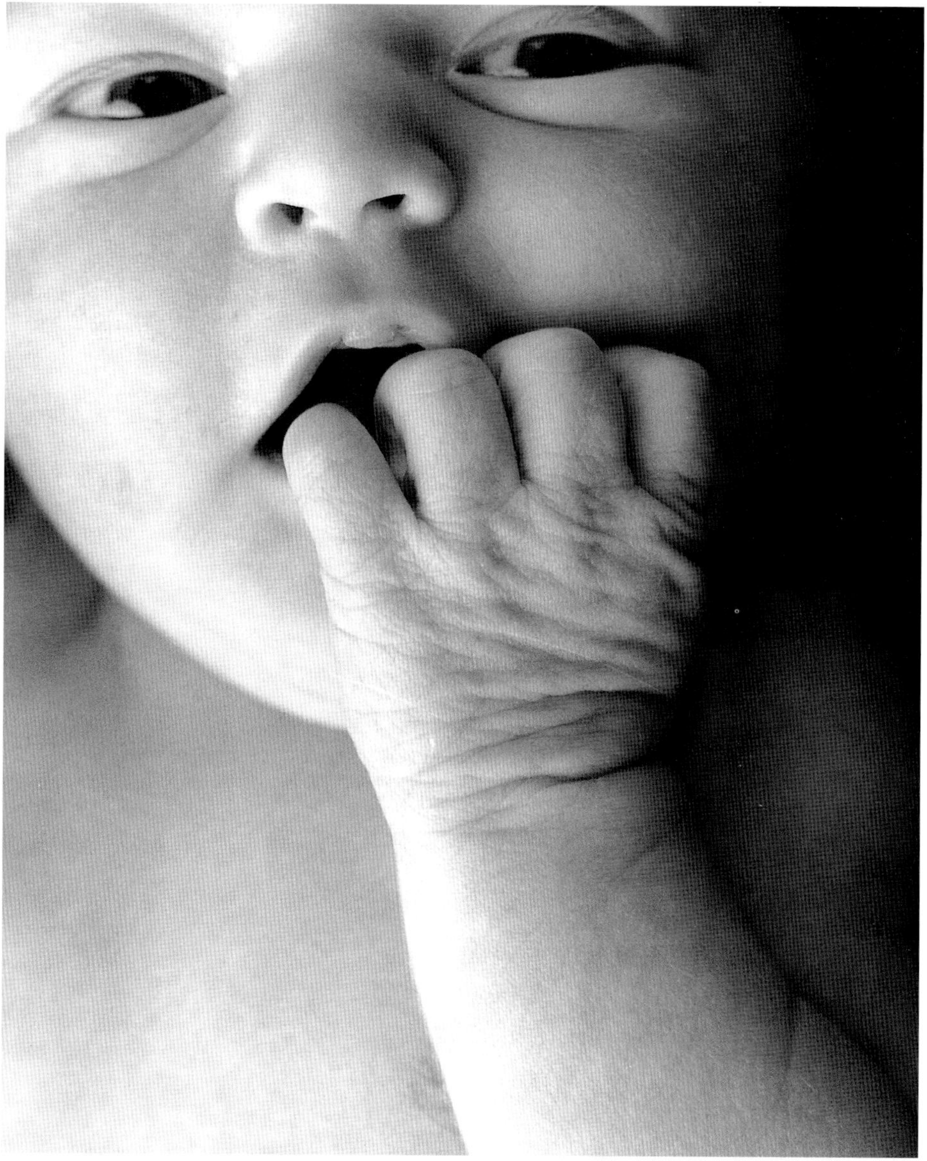

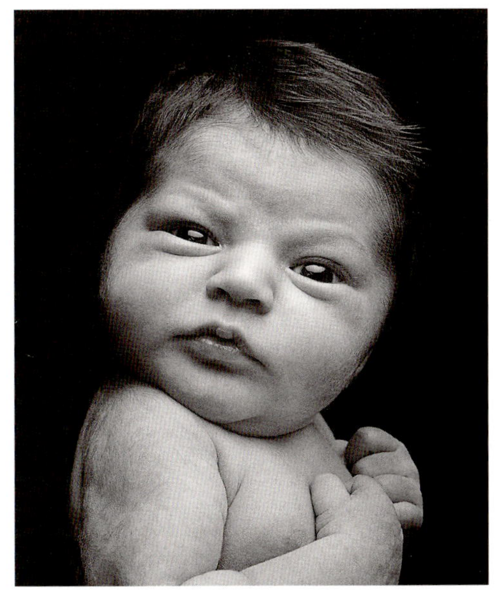

1 day **Ariana**

3 days

Tyler

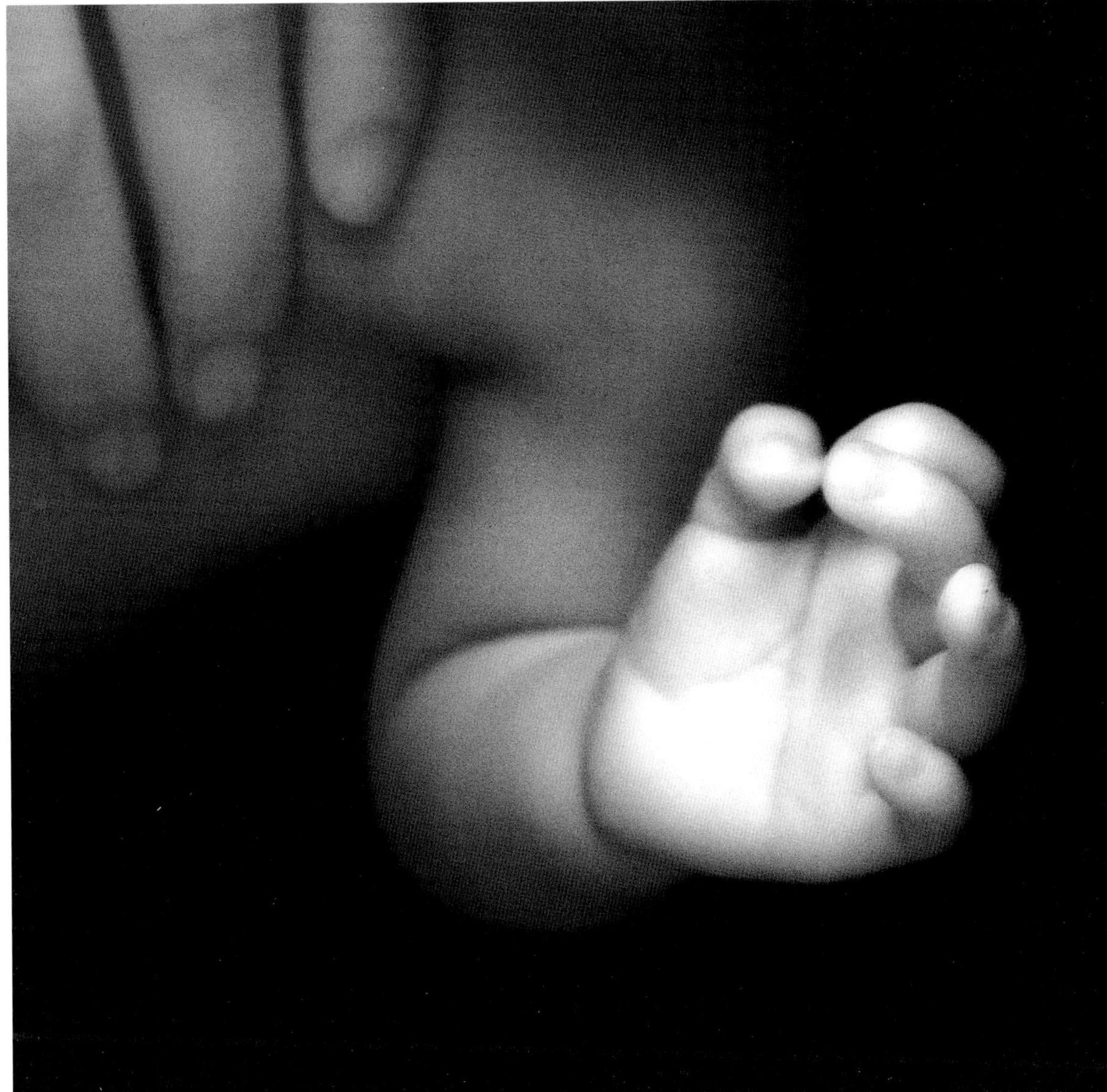

4 days juliette

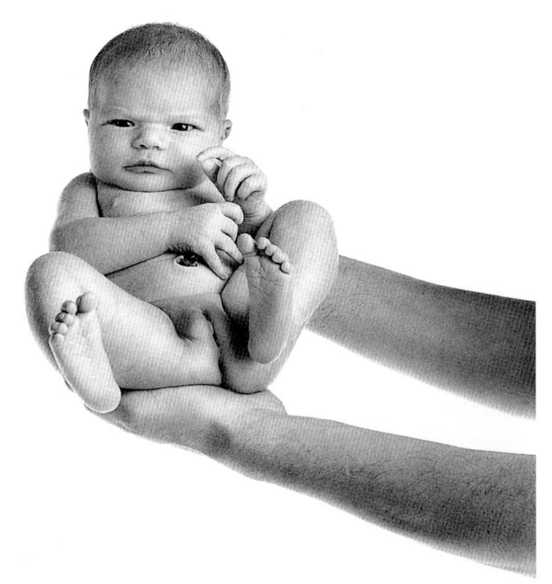

Acknowledgments There are a number of people without whose help this body of work would not have been possible: first and foremost, the one hundred and ten women who shared this most special time in their lives with us. The newborn images constitute one of two parts of this project. The other consists of images of the mothers-to-be, photographed during the last two weeks of their pregnancy; those images are collected in a new book called *Anticipation*, which will also be published in 1996. The generosity of spirit and open approach to this undertaking on the part of all the parents who participated in this project made these wondrous images possible.

Six people in particular helped smooth the path for the majority of the participants in this project and we owe them an enormous debt of gratitude: Dr. Sarah Kilpatrick, University of California, San Francisco Obstetrics/Gynecology Faculty Practice; Erin Carney and Amrit K. Khalsa, both R.N.'s and midwives, the dedicated directors of Labor of Love Midwifery Services in Mill Valley, California; Linda Watson, director of Labor Support Services in San Anselmo, California; Dr. Sylvia Flores, an obstetrician/gynecologist in private practice in San Rafael, California; and Mary Elizabeth Jones, C.R.N.A. (Certified Registered Nurse Anesthetist) at the Gallup Indian Medical Center, who welcomed us into the newborn nursery one hot July afternoon and introduced us to ten Native American women who trundled their newborns down the hall to our makeshift studio—in a few cases, within hours of the birth of their babies.

A number of others helped us by telling their pregnant patients and clients about this project: Dr. Stephen Bearg; Dr. Dorothy Dubé; Dr. David Finkelstein; Dr. David Galland; Nurse-Practitioner Linda Goldberg; Dr. Laurie Green;

Dr. Jordan Horowitz; Kathleen Safford, R.N., Coordinator of U.C.S.F. Antenatal Testing; Dr. Katie Shapiro; Dr. Maida Taylor; Dr. Gerald Wilner. Our grateful thanks to all of them.

Finally, Chris Brown and the president of Calumet Photographic, Kathy Houde, supplied the Balcar units that provided the lighting for this project. We are tremendously appreciative of their generosity. Eileen Healy at Chimera graciously provided the wonderful lightbanks that were used consistently in photographing these newborns. And, as always, Tony Corbell and Chuck Gutierrez of Hasselblad have been steadfast in their support and always generous with their help. This project was shot entirely with a Hasselblad camera.

Beverly Ornstein, Project Director/Editor
January 1996

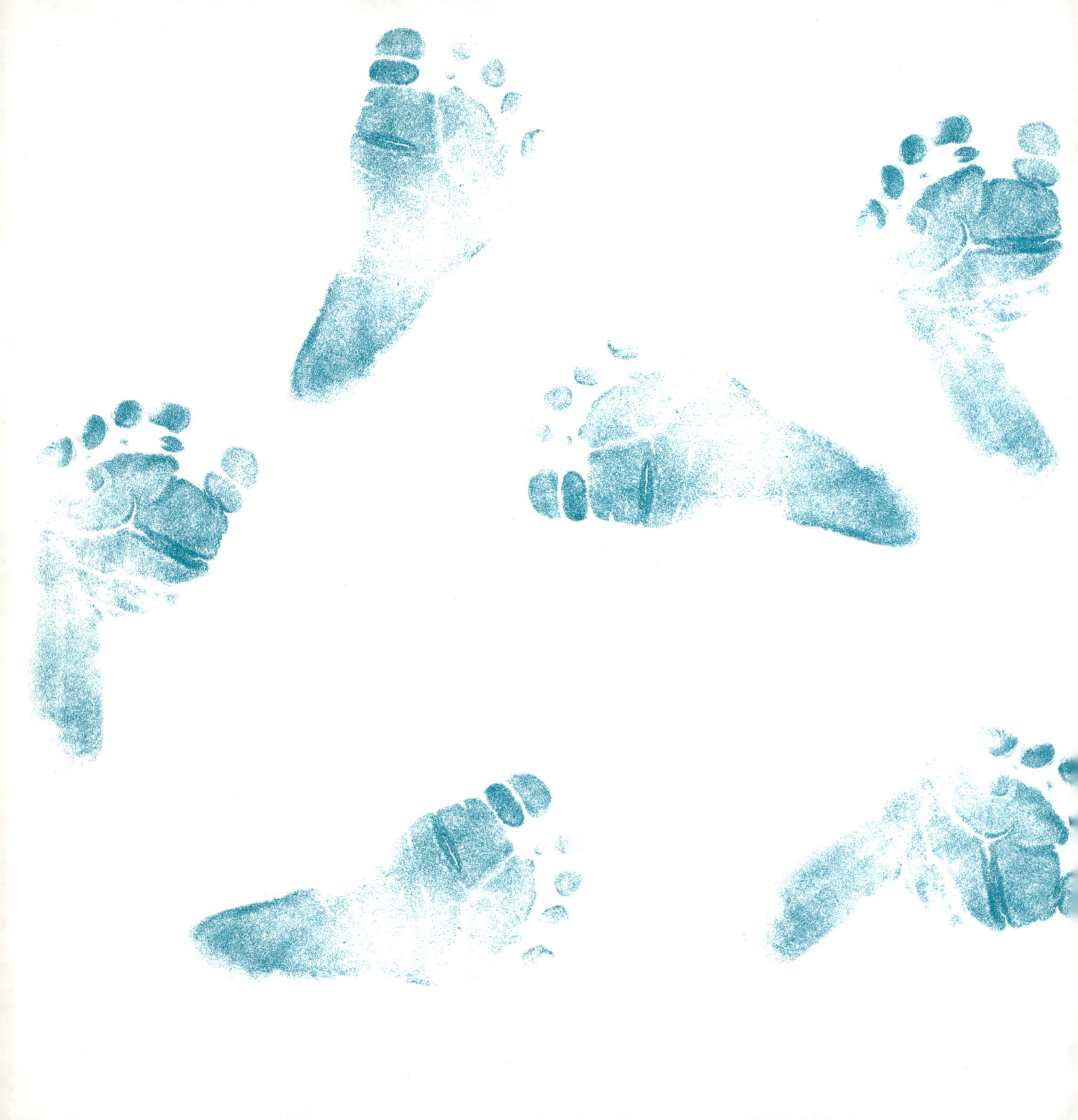